# Best Wishes

*Elmer B. Harris*

# AN ALABAMA LEGACY
*images of a state*

Cherokee Rock Village, located on top of Lookout Mountain, is a "village" consisting of enormous boulders of all shapes and sizes. It offers visitors a thirty-mile view of parts of two states—Alabama and Georgia. (Cherokee County. Photograph by Dan Brothers. Courtesy of the Alabama Bureau of Tourism and Travel.)

# AN ALABAMA LEGACY
*images of a state*

*by Leah Rawls Atkins, William Warren Rogers, and Robert David Ward*

*Alice Knierim, Editor*

# *Stars Fell on Alabama*

*Lyrics by Mitchell Parish*
*Music by Frank Perkins*

*We lived our little drama,
we kissed in a field of white,
and stars fell on Alabama last night.*

*I can't forget the glamour,
your eyes held a tender light,
and stars fell on Alabama last night.*

*I never planned in my imagination
a situation so heavenly
A fairy land where no one else could enter,
and in the center just you and me, dear,*

*My heart beat like a hammer,
my arms wound around you tight,
and stars fell on Alabama last night.*

Buck's Pocket State Park near Grove Oak offers visitors camping and picnic areas, boating, fishing, and hiking trails. In Alabama political lore, Buck's Pocket is the place defeated politicians go to heal their wounds. (DeKalb County. Photograph by Dan Brothers. Courtesy of the Alabama Bureau of Tourism and Travel.)

Library of Congress Cataloging in Publication Data:

Atkins, Leah Rawls.
    An Alabama legacy : images of a state / by Leah Rawls Atkins, William Warren Rogers, and Robert David Ward.
      p.  cm.
Includes biliographical references and index
ISBN 0-89865-950-7 (hc : alk. paper)
1. Alabama--History. 2. Alabama--History--Pictorial works.
I. Rogers, William Warren. II. Ward, Robert David. III. Title
F326.A86 1995
976.1--dc20
Printed in the United States of America

95-36487
CIP

*Stars Fell on Alabama* by Frank Perkins and Mitchell Parish
©1934(Renewed) EMI Mills Music, Inc.
All Rights Reserved    Used by Permission
*Warner Bros. Publications* U.S. Inc. Miami, Fl. 33014

Copyright © 1995 by Leah Rawls Atkins,
William Warren Rogers, and Robert David Ward

All rights reserved, including the right to reproduce this work
in any form whatsoever without permission in writing from the publisher,
except for brief passages in connection with a review. For information, write:

The Donning Company/Publishers
184 Business Park Drive, Suite 106
Virginia Beach, VA 23462

Steve Mull, General Manager
B. L. Walton Jr., Project Director
Laura D. Hill, Research Consultant
Richard A. Horwege, Editor
Chris Decker, Designer
Dawn V. Kofroth, Production Manager
Tony Lillis, Director of Marketing

Swann Covered Bridge near Cleveland is one of thirteen covered bridges in the state. Four of the bridges are in Blount County. (Blount County. Photograph by Dan Brothers. Courtesy of the Alabama Bureau of Tourism and Travel.)

Foreword by Governor Fob James ...6

Acknowledgments ...8

Prologue ...12

Introduction ...13

Chapter one

**Alabama's Early History ...15**

Chapter two

**Statehood and Politics ...19**

Chapter three

**Alabama's Military Heritage ...37**

Chapter four

**Agriculture ...53**

Chapter five

**Transportation ...69**

Chapter six

**Industry ...83**

Chapter seven

**The Growth of Cities ...113**

Chapter eight

**Education ...129**

Chapter nine

**Religion ...147**

Chapter ten

**Leisure ...159**

Chapter eleven

**Family Album ...179**

Chapter twelve

**Conclusion ... 198**

**Bibliography ... 200**

**Index ... 202**

**About the Authors ... 208**

# foreword

Dear Fellow Citizens:

Alabama is truly a wonderful place to live. We are blessed with the richness of our natural resources, the beauty of the land, and the strength and diversity of our citizens. We also are endowed with a unique history forged by the struggles and triumphs, the faith and forbearance of those who have gone before. This historical legacy is a common inheritance shared by all Alabamians. It is the foundation upon which, working together, we will build a bright future.

Alabama's legacy is a priceless resource for each citizen. It is passed down in families from generation to generation through stories, traditions, crafts, shared memories, heirlooms, and family papers. It also is preserved in the collections of records, manuscripts, photographs, and artifacts managed for all Alabamians by archives, libraries, historical societies, and museums across the state.

The Alabama Department of Archives and History plays a vital role in ensuring our state's cultural heritage is preserved for today's citizens and for future generations. The Archives collects, preserves, interprets, and makes accessible the records and artifacts of the government and people of Alabama. The work of the Archives is important to us all. Through it, we honor those Alabamians who preceded us by documenting their lives and contributions to the state and gain a better understanding of how we became who we are today.

The Friends of the Alabama Archives is a membership organization of citizens and businesses across the state who understand the importance of our historical legacy and who support the efforts of the Department of Archives and History to preserve the records and artifacts that tell the story of our state. To promote a better understanding of Alabama history and to share with our citizens the rich, diverse collections of the Archives, the Friends group has published *An Alabama Legacy: Images of a State*. This book captures Alabama in all its varied splendor and documents in words and photographs the struggles, triumphs, and enduring accomplishments of the people who have inhabited this place called Alabama for over ten thousand years.

I commend *An Alabama Legacy* to you. As you turn its pages and lose yourself in the images of the past, perhaps you too will be filled with pride and awe at all our ancestors accomplished and gratitude for the strength and durability of the legacy we proudly carry with us into the twenty-first century.

Sincerely,

Fob James, Governor

# This book is dedicated to
# Judge C.J. Coley

This marker for the site of the Horseshoe Bend Battle Ground was dedicated in June 1951. Judge C. J. Coley, on the far right, was a leading force behind the establishment of the national military park which recognizes the significance of the Battle of Horseshoe Bend in early American history. With Judge Coley, from left to right, were Dr. Ralph B. Draughon, Peter A. Brannon, Marie Bankhead Owen, Hill Ferguson, and Rucker Agee. (Tallapoosa County. ADAH.)

For over thirty-five years as a trustee and thirty years as chairman of the Board of Trustees, Judge Coley has inspired and shaped the development of the Alabama Department of Archives and History. He also has helped preserve our history and promote the understanding of it in countless other ways—through leadership in the Alabama Historical Association, the establishment of Horseshoe Bend National Military Park, his own research and writing, and a lifetime of continued acts of generosity and assistance.

Although this dedication focuses on Judge Coley's efforts in behalf of Alabama history, it is also appropriate to note some of his other contributions: as a leading banker in Alabama for over half a century; as a probate judge for Tallapoosa County; as a founding member of the Alabama Commission on Higher Education; as an alumni leader of the University of Alabama; as the first president of the Alabama 4-H Foundation, Inc.; as a recipient of the prestigious Silver Beaver Award because of his many contributions to scouting; as a worker with recovering alcoholics for over fifty years; and as an active member of the Presbyterian Church in Alexander City and Alabama.

In a remarkable life that reflects the best of Alabama, Judge Coley has lived out the words that he himself uses as the highest possible compliment—he has been and continues to be a "useful citizen."

# acknowledgments

The white sand beaches on the Gulf of Mexico at Gulf Shores are among the most beautiful in the world. (Baldwin County. Photograph by Dan Brothers. Courtesy of the Alabama Bureau of Tourism and Travel.)

The Prologue to this book recounts the day in 1833 when Alabama was showered with thousands of shooting stars. It is our hope that the special quality that imbued Alabama after that spectacle is evident throughout *An Alabama Legacy: Images of a State*. Certainly, a number of very special people came together to make this book possible. Without the enthusiasm, expertise, and generosity of literally dozens of people, the Friends of the Alabama Archives and Department of Archives and History would not have been able to produce this book of which we are so proud.

First, we must thank Leah Rawls Atkins, William Warren Rogers, and Robert David Ward, the authors of *An Alabama Legacy*. Their collective knowledge of Alabama history is astounding and evident in the series of concise essays on important themes in the state's history that introduce each section of the book. These essays make *An Alabama Legacy* a sound history text, as well as an engaging volume of historical photographs. In addition, the authors identified hundreds of photographs from which the final selections for the book were made. We are indebted to their enduring love for our state and their contributions to our knowledge of the past.

Second, this book would not have been attempted without the enthusiastic support of the Board of Directors of the Friends of the Alabama Archives. Under the leadership of Delaine Ray and Judge Bobby Junkins, the Board undertook the challenge of publishing what became a comprehensive photographic history of the state. We wish to acknowledge the members who served on the Board during the nearly three years of planning and realization of this significant project: Dr. Richard Bailey, Dwight Carlisle, Margaret Cowart, J. Mason Davis, Dr. Camille Elebash, George Elliott, Stanhope Elmore, Dr. Janice Franklin, Nimrod Frazer, Dr. Grace

Lake Martin was created in the 1920s when the Alabama Power Company constructed a hydroelectric dam on the Tallapoosa River. Today it is one of the most popular recreational areas in the state. Still Waters Resort on Lake Martin offers golf, tennis, watersports, fishing, backpacking, and bike trails. (Tallapoosa County. Photograph by Dan Brothers. Courtesy of the Alabama Bureau of Tourism and Travel.)

On its way to the confluence with the Alabama River in Dallas County, the Cahaba River flows past Centreville in Bibb County. (Bibb County. Photograph by Dan Brothers. Courtesy of the Alabama Bureau of Tourism and travel.)

Gates, Dr. Cleveland Hammonds, Barrie Harmon, William Bibb Lamar III, Griffin Lassiter, Judge Val McGee, Judge John Moore, Judge William Page, Judge John Patterson, William Powell, Lois Robertson, Sally Spencer, Theda Tankersley, Judge Sam Taylor, Gwyn Turner, Dr. Daniel Williams, Lolla Wright, Milly Wright, Florence Young, and Mary Zoghby.

Shannon Britton, coordinator of the Friends of the Alabama Archives, played a vital role in developing the strategies and materials to market this book on a statewide basis. This extensive effort enabled the Friends and the Archives to communicate with new audiences across the state about the importance of preserving our historical resources.

The Board of Trustees of the Department of Archives and History is a constant source of wisdom and support, and we thank them for embracing this project. Judge C. J. Coley, chairman of the Board of Trustees, is a state treasure and active supporter of this book. We appreciate the encouragement of all the Trustees: George Evans, The Most Rev. Oscar Lipscomb, Shirley McCrary, John Oliver, James Simpson, and Robert E. Steiner III.

The staff of the Department of Archives and History has contributed a tremendous amount of support, expertise, and time to *An Alabama Legacy*. The following staff members supported the book in a variety of ways from reading text and locating and researching photographs to arranging for off-hours access to the building and dry-mounting photographs: Tracey Berezansky, Bob Bradley, Mike Breedlove, Rickie Brunner, Bob Cason, Patricia Clay, Joan Clemens, Margaret Cleveland, Beryl Copeland, Sheila Green, Norwood Kerr, Elizabeth Lee, Alden Monroe, Victor Nielsen, Linda Overman, Mark Palmer, Debbie Pendleton, Pam Richardson, Mary Jo Scott, Deborah Skaggs, Patricia Sweet, Frazine Taylor, Dick Wells, Debra Wilkins, and Tanya Zanish. In

Canning was a necessity in an age that lacked modern methods of preservation and where family food production was the basis of existence. The grocery store and the supermarket changed the pattern of food distribution, but women in rural areas still relied on canning to provide variety to their family's diet. Jorena Pettway, photographed in her smokehouse at Gee's Bend in May 1939, culled peas before beginning the canning process. (Wilcox County. ADAH.)

addition, we want to thank the student aides in reference who facilitated research and the Archives volunteers and junior volunteers who assisted with the marketing campaign. A special thank you goes to Barbara Taylor who worked on marketing and publicity while on the Archives staff—and continued to work on the book even after she transferred to the Alabama Department of Economic and Community Affairs.

The success of a pictorial history is determined by the quality of its photographs. Approximately two-thirds of the images in *An Alabama Legacy* are from the collections of the Department of Archives and History, and many of them are published here for the first time. All photographs from the Archives are identified in the captions by ADAH. The remaining photographs generously were made available to us by fifty-seven repositories and individuals across the state. Any list is subject to errors, and we want to apologize to anyone inadvertently left off this list. However, we do want to acknowledge publicly those people who have enthusiastically supported this project and often made possible the seemingly impossible. They include: Dan Brothers, Alabama Bureau of Tourism and Travel; Meg Crawford, Alabama Cattlemen's Association; Joan Young and Beverly Helsel, Alabama Constitution Village; Mark Morrison, Alabama Farm Federation; Kim Gilliland, Alabama Forestry Commission; Claudia Cumming, Alabama Museum of Natural History, University of Alabama; Victor Wheeler, Alabama Power Company; Bill Tharpe, Alabama Power Company Corporate Archives; Griffin Lassiter, Alabama Resource Center; Minnie Wood, Alabama State University Library; Ethelda Potts and Marilyn Steens, Aliceville Public Library; Bonnie Seymour, Public Library of Anniston and Calhoun County; Dwayne Cox and Bev Powers, Auburn University Archives; Leah Rawls Atkins, Jay Lamar, and Serlester Williams, Auburn University Center for the Arts and Humanities; and the Auburn University Photographic Services.

Our thanks also go to: Rus Baxley; the *Birmingham News*; Marvin Whiting, Jim Baggett, and Don Veasey, Birmingham Public Library Department of Archives and Manuscripts; Joe Dickson, the *Birmingham World*; Ken Geddy and Taylor Watson, Paul W. Bryant Museum, University of Alabama; Herbert Carter; Judge C. J. Coley; Shirley Spears, B. B. Comer Memorial Library; Custom Photo Art, Birmingham; the Demopolis Public Library; Mary Davis Elmore; Robert Fouts and Mikki Keenan, Fouts Commercial Photography, Montgomery; the Hightower Photograph Committee; Hugh Terry and Andrea Watson, William Stanley Hoole Special Collections Library, University of Alabama; Bettye Forbus and Anne McKee of the Houston Love Memorial Library; Raneé Pruitt and Denise Terry, Huntsville-Madison County Public Library; Henry Joe; James R. Kuykendall and Collins Kirby, Landmarks of DeKalb County, Inc.; the Library of Congress; Henry and Betty McAdory; Eloise McClendon; John McFarland; Joe C. P. Turner, Gwyn Turner, and Denise Milton, Marengo County Historical Society; Hubert Matthews; and the Monroe Public Library.

We also appreciate the cooperation of: Lynn Williamson Weissman and William Brown, the *Montgomery Advertiser*; Doug Purcell; the Old Depot Museum in Selma; Bill Niblett, Opp Public Library; Elizabeth Wells, Special Collection, Samford University Library; Flora Maye Simmons; George Elliott, Deborah Hughes, and Joy James, BellSouth; Carl and Jesse Summers; Will Hill Tankersley; David Taylor, Sunbelt Golf Corporation; Dan Williams, Tuskegee University Archives; Regina Burns, U.S. Army Aviation Museum; Gretchen Greeson, U.S. Army Corps of Engineers; Michael Baker, U.S. Army Missile Command, Redstone Arsenal; Michael Thomason and Elisa Baldwin, University of South Alabama Archives; Margene Walker; Mickey Watkins; Sallie Riehl and Margarete Lange, Wheeler Basin Regional Library; the Wilcox County Library; Kathryn Tucker Windham; and Cecelia Zimmerman.

Finally, we would like to thank Bernie Walton, Betsy Bobbitt, Richard Horwege, Tony Lillis, Teri Arnold, and the staff of the Donning Company/Publishers who have been so helpful and patient throughout the long process of bringing the dream of this book to reality.

We hope you enjoy
*An Alabama Legacy : Images of a State!*
Alice Knierim, Editor
Edwin C. Bridges, Director
Department of Archives and History

# prologue

Early on the morning of Wednesday, November 13, 1833, the sky over Alabama suddenly came alive with brilliant lights that sparkled and darted around, and it seemed as if all the stars in the heavens were showering down to earth. People ran outside to gaze in wonder and awe at the glorious but fearful sights as hundreds, then thousands, of shooting stars rained down for over two hours. Some cried that "the end of the earth is at hand," and no one who saw it could ever forget. From that time on events were remembered as before or after the stars fell on Alabama. Carl Carmer, a New Yorker who lived in Alabama in the 1920s and wrote about his experiences when he returned north, believed the stars changed the land's destiny and made it a land of enchantment like no other place on earth. Most Alabamians would agree.

The people of Alabama are diverse—white, black, Native American, Asian—natives and recent immigrants. The terrain is as varied as the people—from pine-covered mountains that roll along the blue horizon in north Alabama to red clay hills with rock outcroppings that hide marble, iron ore, coal, and gold; from cool valleys with bubbling springs and brooks to Black Belt plains with dark loamy soil where cotton once grew and in early fall turned the landscape white as far as the eye could see; from flat coastal plains, where coarse wiregrass sprouted in the east and pine barrens stretched to the west, to musty swamps with ceilings of moss and muddy rivers that extend from the hills like highways; from fine white sand Gulf beaches to deep blue-green lakes.

Alabama is indeed a special place, a land of enchantment with a past that has been entwined with the chronicle of the American nation. Life in Alabama has reflected the experiences of other Americans or Southerners, but Alabamians also have a history that uniquely belongs to our state.

Two-thirds of Alabama is covered with forests, 95 percent of which are privately owned. Alabama forests directly provide employment for over 66,000 people, supporting over 62,000 workers in manufacturing alone. Trees not only provide an income for Alabamians, they also provide a home for wildlife and a recreational area to hunt, fish, hike, and picnic. (Wilcox County. Photograph by Dr. Hubert I. Matthews. Courtesy of the Alabama Forestry Commission.)

# introduction

The past surrounds Alabama's citizens, permeating their lives and giving substance and meaning to the present. Photographs allow a view of past times and places and people that words cannot evoke. They are a brief moment in history, frozen for later viewing. Through photographs the continuity of life in Alabama is spread out and observable in all its complexity and splendid variety.

Historical photographs illustrate that life in Alabama has changed as the decades and centuries have passed and as technology has altered the way men and women accomplish life's tasks. Mules and plows give way to tractors and combines. Creek fordings and ferry crossings have almost disappeared as bridges, big and small, cross the water highways of the past. Wagons are replaced by railroads. The stern- and side-wheeler boats that once steamed up and down the state's rivers carrying merchandise to towns and farms and cotton to market have been displaced by diesel tugs pushing or pulling barges loaded with coal or iron ore or by eighteen-wheel tractor-trailer trucks rolling over concrete interstate highways.

Although technology has transformed the landscape and altered the way Alabamians live and work, the essential forms of humanity have not changed. Tradition, ritual, and faith are as important in Alabama today as they were two hundred years ago. The sense of place and family that permeates the stories of the state's writers remains strong. Lessons of courage and perseverance, faith and forbearance, hope and acceptance emerge from the forge of history to link Alabamians of the past to those of the present. Upon the foundation laid brick by brick, year after year, by its people—men and women with skin hues of red, white, almond, black, and brown—the state has been built.

Just as the past has shaped today, the present will shape tomorrow. *An Alabama Legacy: Images of a State* is more than a pictorial and narrative effort to tell the story of Alabama; it is a tribute to those who built that common past upon which Alabamians today, working together, can build a future of promise and fulfillment.

A highlight of DeSoto State Park is DeSoto Falls, a beautiful 100-foot waterfall on the West Fork of Little River. (DeKalb County. Photograph by Dan Brothers. Courtesy of the Alabama Bureau of Tourism and Travel.)

In 1909, a group of Montgomerians founded the Alabama Anthropological Society to study the remnants of Indian culture in central Alabama. These amateur archaeologists spent the next three decades researching historical sources, locating mounds and village sites, and, especially, collecting artifacts. At first they limited their fieldwork to hunting the surfaces of plowed fields, but soon Society members began to excavate. Although their techniques were quite destructive by today's standards, members did keep careful notes on their work that have been valuable to modern archaeologists and added to our knowledge of early Indian life. Members of the Alabama Anthropological Society included Thomas M. Owen Jr. who was the first director of the Alabama Department of Archives and History, Peter A. Brannon who became the third director of the Archives, J. Y. Brame, Buckner Beasley, James M. White Sr., H. H. Paulin, and John K. McEwen Sr. On July 21, 1912, members gathered at Manack near Pintlala Creek for the annual meeting of the Society. (Montgomery County. ADAH.)

# one
## *Alabama's Early History*

Caves in Alabama were the homes of aboriginal men and women who inhabited the area as long as ten thousand years ago. Archaeologists have chronicled the development of this native culture through various stages and eras, which culminated in the highly advanced Late Mississippian civilization. Europeans who came to explore Alabama in the sixteenth century encountered these Indians.

The intrusion of Europeans shocked the world of the Alabama Indians. The explorers introduced new weapons, alien ideas, and strange diseases for which the native inhabitants had no immunity. Although often peaceful, early exploration in Alabama also produced conflict. On October 18, 1540, the expedition of Spanish explorer Hernando de Soto engaged Chief Tascaluza and his tribe at their capital, Mabila, the exact location of which remains one of the state's great mysteries. The six hundred Spanish conquistadores here withstood an estimated ten thousand Indians in what was the largest battle ever fought between explorers and Indians in North America.

For a century and a half following this bloody encounter, Europeans made few ventures into the land soon to be called Alabama, named for the Alabamas

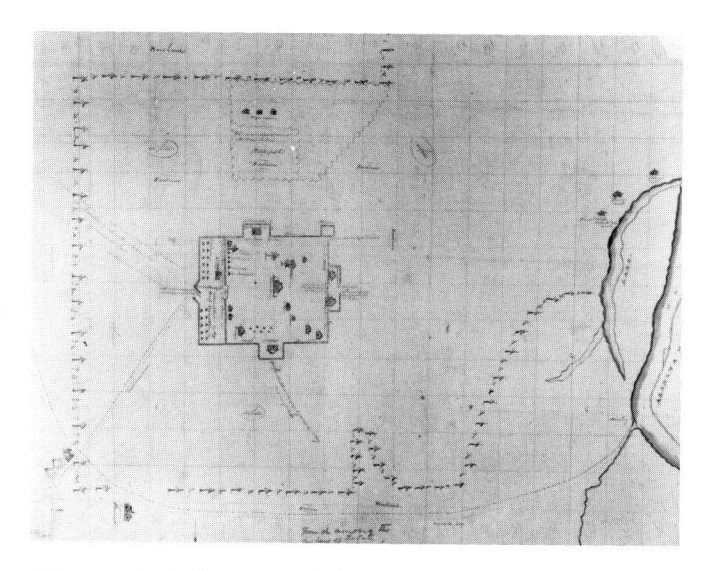

When hostile Creeks threatened the frontier around Tensaw, settlers gathered at Samuel Mims' house which was enclosed by a high stockade hastily constructed for security. The militia at the fort was under the command of Major Daniel Beasley, an inexperienced military officer who ignored warnings of the pending attack. The Indians attacked on August 30, 1813, killing at least 250 people. This map was drawn as part of a report after the "Fort Mims Massacre." (Baldwin County. Map from the collections of the ADAH.)

Indians who lived along the great river that flowed a winding course across the south. Exploration and colonization began in earnest in 1702 with the French settlement on Dauphin Island and, twenty miles up the Mobile River, at Fort Louis. Meanwhile, remnants of the Mississippian culture had evolved into new groups—tribes known as Choctaw, Chickasaw, Cherokee, and Creek. Disease and conflict had decimated their people, and the native cultures of the 1700s lacked the technology and strength of numbers to defend themselves against the relentless forces of European occupation and settlement.

In the eighteenth century, imperial rivalry among the powers of Europe—Spain, France, and England—and their American colonies laced the Alabama frontier with intrigue and conflict. Ultimately a new country, the United States of America, acquired permanent control of the area, in part an outcome of that European rivalry.

When the U.S. government cut the Federal Road through Creek lands in eastern Alabama, new conflicts with the Indians erupted and became a regional manifestation of the War of 1812. The Indians struggled to prevent their lands from being taken by the Americans, who, in turn, considered the Indians obstacles to settlement. The Creeks defeated the militia at Burnt Corn Creek in what is now Escambia County in July 1813, and on August 30, 1813, they attacked Fort Mims in present-day Baldwin County, killing at least 250 occupants who had taken refuge there.

Other encounters followed. The Battle of Holy Ground in present Lowndes County on December 23, 1813, ended in victory for the Americans. On March 27, 1814, Andrew Jackson and his Tennessee Volunteer Militia, together with other forces including some Indians, attacked the Creeks at their encampment on the Tallapoosa River and won the hard-fought engagement. The Battle of Horseshoe Bend was decisive in breaking the power of the Upper Creek confederacy, and the victory made Jackson a national hero. Afterwards, the Treaty of Fort Jackson opened much of Alabama for settlement.

Settlers from Tennessee and from the Piedmont and Seaboard South rushed to the region to claim land vacated by the Indians. These pioneers walked, rode in carts or on horseback, and carried upon mules or in wagons all the supplies needed for a life in the wilderness. Often the fording places at creeks were so congested that caravans had to wait their turn to cross. Word spread back east that Alabama was a healthy place with plenty of fresh water and fertile soil. And more people came.

Andrew Jackson, who commanded the Tennessee militia to victory against the hostile Creek Nation, became a national hero at the Battle of Horseshoe Bend. Jackson enjoyed a strong political following in Alabama throughout the rest of his lifetime. This portrait of Jackson was painted by Ralph Eleaser Whiteside Earl prior to 1826. Earl, an artist who worked in New Orleans between 1821 and 1837, was related to Jackson by marriage and devoted himself to painting portraits of the president. He was listed as "artist in residence" at the Hermitage, Jackson's home in Nashville, at the time of the Marquis de LaFayette's visit in 1825. This portrait of Jackson, "painted from life at the Hermitage," was the painting upon which Charles C. Torrey based a widely circulated engraving. (Portrait from the collections of the ADAH.)

William Wyatt Bibb, the first governor of Alabama, selected the site for the new Alabama capital at the confluence of the Alabama and Cahaba Rivers. Named Cahawba, the town grew into a thriving community with a school, hotels, boardinghouses, and two newspapers. In the fall of 1820, the legislature met there for the first time. Unfortunately, rains, floods, and outbreaks of the "bilious remitting disease," later identified as yellow fever, struck the city in 1821 and 1822. Caught in regional competition and its reputation damaged beyond repair, Cahawba was abandoned by the legislature for a new capital in Tuscaloosa. Cahawba continued to thrive as a Dallas County river town; however, when the county seat was relocated to Selma, it began to decline. By the end of the nineteenth century, all that was left of the former capital was the cemetery and a few buildings. This photograph of Vine Street between Capital Avenue and South Street was taken circa 1890. The tall building on the right was the courthouse. On the back of another picture of the courthouse from the same collection is written: "Used as Millhouse, and irony of Fate, Corn is now ground in its old rooms of State! Where the eloquence of Yancey and Murphy burst forth, No sound can be heard but the Miller's rude oath!" (Dallas County. ADAH.)

# two
*Statehood and Politics*

Democratic societies make their decisions and choose their course through politics. The uneven, often acrimonious, process of politics provides a continuous thread through the state's history and affords one way to view Alabama. After Congress created the Alabama Territory on March 3, 1817, and made St. Stephens the capital, President James Monroe appointed William Wyatt Bibb of Georgia the territorial governor. Growth was so rapid that the territorial legislature met for only two sessions before the expanding population exceeded the requisite number needed for statehood.

Congress passed an enabling act, which allowed the people of Alabama to form a state government. Bibb was elected Alabama's first governor, and the state legislature convened at Huntsville, where Alabama's first constitution was written. Congress recognized these efforts on December 14, 1819, admitting Alabama as the twenty-second state in the Union.

Huntsville was only a temporary seat of government, and in 1820 the Alabama capitol was completed in the new town of Cahawba (whose spelling was later changed to match that of the river). This site at the confluence of the Cahaba and Alabama Rivers was to become the permanent seat

STATE HOUSE, TUSCALOOSA, AL.

When the Alabama capital was moved to Tuscaloosa in 1826, the legislature commissioned William Nichols to design an appropriate building. The structure was completed in 1829 and housed state government until 1846 when the decision was made to move the capital to Montgomery. (Tuscaloosa County. Courtesy of the William Stanley Hoole Special Collections Library, University of Alabama.)

of government provided it proved to be a satisfactory location during the next five years. But the low-lying area was plagued with fever and floods, and in 1826 the capital was moved to Tuscaloosa, where it remained for twenty years. This location, too, proved unsatisfactory. Summer droughts caused low water in the Warrior River and often prevented travel as far north as Tuscaloosa. Rapid growth of the southern cotton areas increased demands that the capital be relocated in a more central and southern area. After a spirited battle in 1846, the legislature selected Montgomery as the fourth site of the state's capital.

In the early years of statehood, partisan politics and political parties emerged. Most early Alabamians allied themselves with the Democratic-Republican Party of Thomas Jefferson, and later they were strongly influenced by Andrew Jackson, who gave American politics an egalitarian cast. The Whigs emerged as a rival party in the 1830s and were perceived as more aristocratic—the party of large planters and commercial interests. Although never able to elect a governor or carry a statewide race, the Whigs won some legislative and congressional seats.

Political battles between the Democrats and

In 1846, when the legislature decided to move the state capital from Tuscaloosa to Montgomery, construction began on a Greek Revival building located on Goat Hill to accommodate state government. This building, designed by Stephen D. Button, burned on December 14, 1849. The fire, which completely destroyed the Capitol, started in the House of Representatives when the legislature was in session. The legislature continued in session in Montgomery with state government housed in various buildings around town. Despite some suggestions that the capital be moved to another town, the legislature refused to change the location again. Instead, $60,000 was appropriated to rebuild the Capitol which was completed by 1851. (Montgomery County. Drawing from the collections of the ADAH.)

The new statehouse was constructed largely on the foundations of the burned building. Portions of the walls of the original Capitol may still be seen beneath the portico of the present building. While elements of the 1846 Button plan were reintroduced in the 1851 building, the final design seems largely to have been the result of committee planning. Daniel Pratt, master-builder turned industrialist, played a major role on the commission formed for rebuilding the Capitol. The principal contractors were John P. Figh and James D. Randolph, and the superintending architect was Barachias Holt. Many furnishings, including most of those in the House and Senate chambers, were rescued from the destroyed statehouse and reused in the new building. This stereograph provides an early view of the new Capitol building. Stereographs were popular photographic forms from 1851 to 1935. Stereo cards consist of a pair of identical photographs placed side by side, which, when viewed through a hand-held stereoscope, appear three-dimensional. (Montgomery County. ADAH.)

In 1860, with agitation for secession growing in the Southern states, the Alabama legislature passed a resolution calling for the election of a convention to consider leaving the Union. Governor A. B. Moore called the election on December 24, 1860, and the elected delegates met in Montgomery on January 7, 1861. A vote on secession was finally taken on January 11. With sixty-one delegates in favor and thirty-nine opposed, Alabama made the fateful decision to leave the Union. The Ordinance also invited representatives of other seceding states to meet in Montgomery, the result of which was the formation of the Confederate States of America. (Document from the collection of the ADAH.)

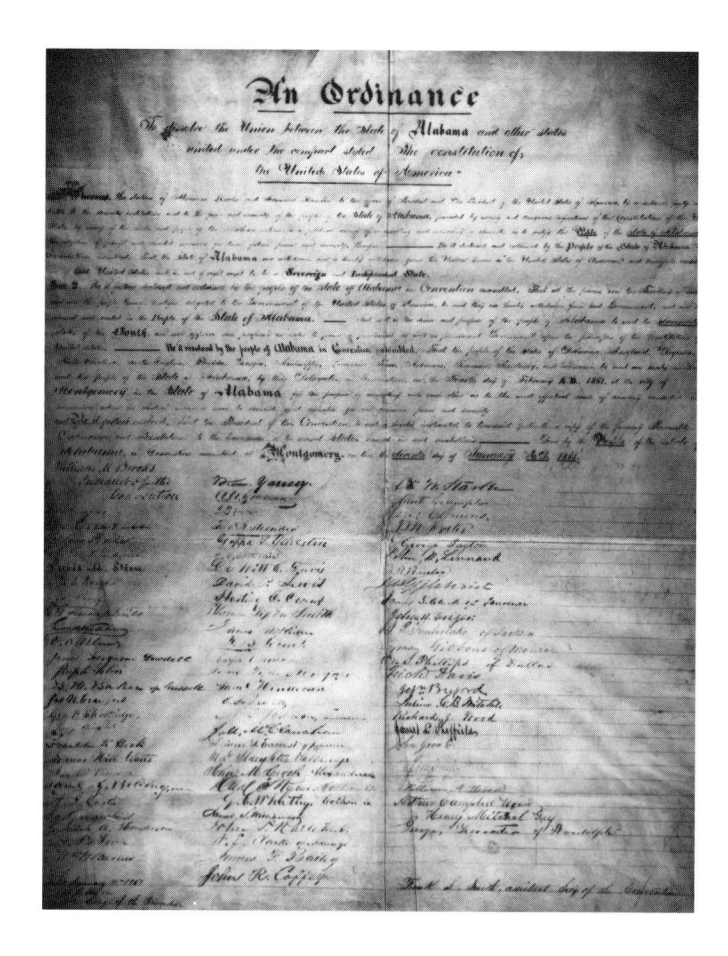

Right: Gaineswood, built at Demopolis by the planter General Nathan Bryan Whitfield, is one of Alabama's premier antebellum mansions. The Greek Revival–style mansion, called Marlmont until 1856, is made of brick and covered with stucco. The house evolved circa 1842–1860 from an earlier structure on the site and was the center of the 480-acre Whitfield estate. The state of Alabama purchased the house in 1966 and restored it as a house museum. (Marengo County. ADAH.)

Left: This is the only known photograph of the inauguration of Jefferson Davis as president of the Confederate States of America on February 18, 1861. Montgomery photographer A. C. MacIntyre recorded the ceremony that took place on the portico of the Capitol. The carriage in the foreground is reputed to be that of Mrs. Sophie Gilmer Bibb who is thought to be one of the two women standing to the right of the carriage. After the Civil War, Mrs. Bibb was instrumental in organizing the Ladies Memorial Association to perpetuate the memory of the Lost Cause. (Montgomery County. ADAH.)

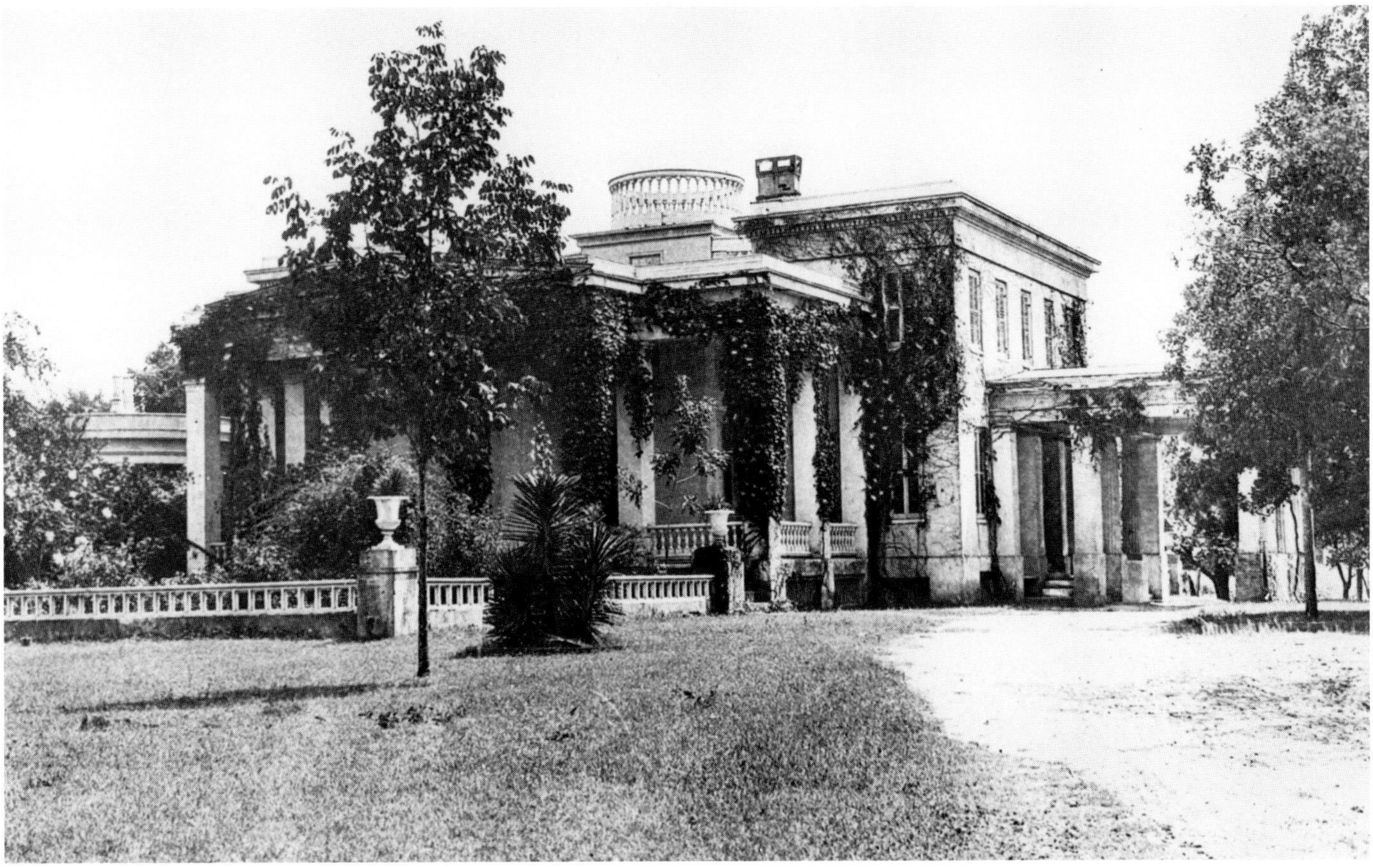

Benjamin Sterling Turner was born a slave in North Carolina. He and a younger brother were moved to Dallas County as children by Mrs. Elizabeth Turner. Young Turner secretly learned how to read and made himself an invaluable servant to Dr. James T. Gee, owner of the St. James Hotel in Selma. After the Civil War, Turner set up his own livery stable and quickly became the wealthiest black man in Dallas County. In 1868, he was elected county tax collector and Selma city councilman. Two years later, he won election as Alabama's first black congressman. During his two years in the U.S. House of Representatives, Turner fought for civil rights for both freedmen and disfranchised Confederate leaders. "The people of Selma have been magnanimous toward me," he said, "and I intend to stand by and labor for them in their need and desolation." Republican intrigues brought about Turner's defeat for re-election in 1872. He returned to Selma, where he was active in community affairs until his death in 1894. He is buried in Old Live Oak Cemetery. (Dallas County. ADAH.)

Whigs made Alabama a two-party state before the Civil War, though by 1856 the Whigs had disintegrated under the pressure of the slavery debate.

In the momentous presidential election of 1860, the Democrats divided nationally into Northern and Southern wings. The Republican ticket did not even appear on the state ballot, and the Southern Democrats prevailed in Alabama. But the Republican candidate, Abraham Lincoln, won the White House. Many Southerners viewed the election as the climax to long-festering sectional rivalries over slavery, land and banking policies, and the tariff. The South, already a minority section within the Congress, saw the Republican Party as a grave threat to its status in the Union. White Southerners feared that the controversy over slavery in the territories might under Lincoln lead to its prohibition in those states where it legally existed.

Defeating the Republicans in 1874 in a violent, racially divisive election campaign, the Conservative Democratic Party summoned a constitutional convention to replace the Republican constitution of 1867. With the old Confederate leadership back in power, many of the social and political changes of the Reconstruction government ended or were reversed. (Montgomery County. ADAH.)

In a highly charged emotional atmosphere, Alabama seceded from the Union on January 11, 1861, and the next month joined with other Southern states in a convention meeting in Montgomery to form a new nation, the Confederate States of America. For four months, Montgomery served as the capital of the Confederacy. The federal government refused to accept the legality of secession or the sovereignty of the Confederate nation. Four years of armed conflict, the tragedy of civil war, followed.

After the war ended in 1865, Alabama went through a period of Reconstruction. The Republican Party was organized in the state, and Alabama was readmitted to the Union in June 1868. The Republicans, however shakily, controlled Alabama until 1874 when George Smith Houston was elected. When the Democrats regained power they held it, and no Republican governor was elected again until Guy Hunt won the office in 1986. For almost a century, Alabama was overwhelmingly Democratic at every level of public office.

Third parties, such as the Independents and the Greenbackers, challenged the Democrats from time to time in the last half of the nineteenth century; however, the only serious threat to their control came

President Woodrow Wilson visited Mobile in October 1913 and attended a breakfast meeting at the Battle House. In his "Mobile Address," Wilson spoke of a day when Latin America would be free of foreign control and indirectly stated that his own intervention in Mexican affairs was to aid the cause of constitutional government. (Mobile County. Courtesy of the University of South Alabama Archives.)

from the Populists in the 1890s. The Populists drew their strength from organized labor and the yeoman and poor farmers, particularly members of the Farmers' Alliance. They also had the support of the Republicans. The Populists argued that the Democrats, known at this time as the Bourbon Democrats, ran the state for the benefit of Black Belt planters and North Alabama bankers, railroad owners, industrialists, and mine operators. Because Black Belt landowners controlled their tenant farmers economically, they also were able to control them politically. If other means were needed to ensure a Democratic victory, the region's county officials and courthouse bosses resorted to stuffing ballot boxes, throwing away opposition ballots, voting the dead, and employing other creative deceptions.

The Alabama Constitution of 1901, which replaced the Constitution of 1875, destroyed the Populist base of support by disfranchising most black voters and eventually a large number of poor whites as well. The system of segregation, which had been evolving over the previous decades, was consolidated under the Constitution of 1901. The Black Belt Democrats, plus the capitalists of North Alabama, who later were known as "Big Mules," cooperated to dominate Alabama politics into the first half of the twentieth century. The 1901 Constitution, amended hundreds of times and with many provisions voided by federal statutes and federal court decisions, remains the state's basic document of government.

Through the first half of the twentieth century Democratic control was scarcely challenged, and the state routinely voted Democratic at the national level. However conservative the politics at home, the state's congressional delegation took leadership roles in Washington, supporting the progressive reforms of Democratic presidents, such as Woodrow Wilson

At the first state convention of the Alabama Equal Suffrage Association (AESA) in 1913, Pattie Ruffner Jacobs was elected president. The group adopted the motto: "We mean to make Alabama lead the South for Woman's Suffrage." To that end, AESA members staffed a booth for woman's suffrage at the 1914 State Fair in Birmingham. Despite their efforts, the Alabama legislature refused to ratify the Nineteenth Amendment until after it already had become part of the United States Constitution in 1920. (Jefferson County. ADAH.)

and Franklin D. Roosevelt. Alabama senators and congressmen were some of the most influential exponents of New Deal legislation, most of which greatly benefited the state. The New Deal programs solidified the party's support in Alabama, but disaffection increased when Harry S Truman pushed civil rights legislation and national Democrats seemed to court urban minorities in northern cities at the expense of white Southerners. In 1948, Alabama joined other lower South states and cast its electoral votes for the States' Rights or "Dixiecrat" Party.

Thomas M. Owen was the first director of the Alabama Department of Archives and History, serving in that capacity from 1901 until his death in 1920. Established in 1901, the Alabama Archives was the first state-funded archival agency in the United States and predated the National Archives by some thirty years. Dr. Owen is shown in his office in the House chamber in the Capitol. During the early 1900s, the legislature met only once every four years. Between sessions, both the Senate and House chambers functioned as museum spaces for the Department of Archives and History. Largely through the persistence and influence of Marie Bankhead Owen, Thomas Owen's widow and successor as director of the Archives, the present Archives and History building was constructed with WPA (Works Progress Administration) funds and completed in 1940. (Montgomery County. ADAH.)

In the 1920s, the Ku Klux Klan again became a factor in Alabama politics and often elected county sheriffs and mayors of cities. Supporting white supremacy and encouraging anti-Catholicism and anti-Semitism, the Klan attracted a large membership. Members often paraded through cities in public displays of organizational strength. Politically, the Klan supported better roads and more money for schools, worked against the convict-lease system, and to some extent became a political voice for many poor white Alabamians. In 1926, Bibb Graves was elected governor of Alabama with Klan support. In 1927, Graves pushed for creation of the Alabama Special Education Trust Fund to earmark certain taxes for schools, and the state outlawed the corrupt convict-lease system. At the height of the Klan's power, however, a popular backlash against the group grew out of reports of its excesses. By ignoring the laws of the state and the rights of its citizens to due process, the Klan rapidly lost membership. By 1930, its influence in state politics had faded once again, as it had after the end of Reconstruction. (Montgomery County. ADAH.)

Women's clubs, such as the Shawhan Parliamentary Practice Club in Mobile, often made conscious efforts to train their members in the substance and techniques of public affairs. (Mobile County. Courtesy of the University of South Alabama Archives.)

*28*

Above: Lister Hill of Montgomery was elected to the U.S. Senate in 1938 after strong New Deal service in the House of Representatives. Hill served in the U.S. Congress for a total of forty-five years, longer than any other Alabamian. He played a key role in more than eighty pieces of major legislation, including the Tennessee Valley Authority, the federal student-loan program, the United Nations, and the Hill-Burton hospital construction program which resulted in almost three hundred new health facilities in Alabama alone. With his Huntsville colleague John Sparkman, Hill was a powerful voice for Alabama liberalism. However, during his career he met with persistent opposition at home, and the rising tide of racial animosity in the state gave Hill only a narrow reelection in 1962. That victory was described "as the last hurrah for the New Deal alliance." Hill retired from the Senate after his term expired in 1968. On May 18, 1933, Senator Hill, standing fourth from the right, watched as President Franklin D. Roosevelt signed the Morris-Hill Bill authorizing the Tennessee Valley Authority. (Washington, D.C. ADAH.)

Governor Bibb Graves appointed his wife, Dixie, to fill Hugo Black's seat in the U.S. Senate after President Franklin D. Roosevelt appointed Black to the Supreme Court. When Dixie Graves was sworn in as a member of the Senate on August 20, 1937, she became the first Alabama woman to sit in the U.S. Senate. Mrs. Graves received the oath of office from Vice-president John Nance Garner while Governor Graves watched from the background and Senator John Bankhead stood to her left. (Washington, D.C. ADAH.)

Into the twentieth century, counties remained seats of power in state political struggles as "courthouse gangs" competed for state influence. The Bullock County Courthouse, circa 1934, was one of many courthouses across the state renovated as a project of the Civil Works Administration (CWA), one of many federal relief programs designed to put unemployed Americans to work during the Great Depression. (Bullock County. ADAH.)

The CWA provided jobs and sponsored educational programs for citizens, contributing to improved skills for Alabama workers. This 1934 first-aid class in Evergreen was a CWA project. (Conecuh County. ADAH.)

Many CWA projects were construction jobs that improved the quality of life in towns and for all Alabamians. Across the state, schools and public buildings were painted and repaired. In towns like Gadsden, new sewer lines were installed. In several counties, levees were strengthened to control floods. In 1933–1934, Fayette County benefited from the construction of this culvert on the Bankston-Eldridge Road. (Fayette County. ADAH.)

*30*

Chauncey Sparks (on the right), a Eufaula attorney and banker, lost the governor's race to Birmingham attorney Frank Dixon in 1938. He rebounded to defeat James Folsom in 1942 in Folsom's first attempt at the office. Sparks, conservative and anti-labor in his campaigns, sponsored tax revision and the extension of social programs when in office. (ADAH.)

By the presidential election of 1952, when Alabama senator John Sparkman of Huntsville was the vice-presidential candidate on the Democratic ticket, and the election of 1956, many Alabamians openly called themselves Democrats for Eisenhower. On a national level, the Republican Party seemed to reflect the business interests of the South, as well as white Southerners' ideas on military and social issues. As the civil rights movement gathered momentum in the late 1950s, the Republican Party profited from white reaction and became a viable threat to the party of the fathers.

The Republicans would have gained wider support even earlier had it not been for the strong personality of George C. Wallace. First, as the Democratic governor and then as a third-party candidate for president, the Barbour County native won the support of a majority of the state's voters in four different campaigns for governor, not including the 1968 campaign in which his wife, Lurleen, was elected. At the end of the twentieth century, with the hard evidence of election returns at every level, Alabama undeniably had become a two-party state.

Addictive though politics may be, most Alabamians have been far more concerned with family and personal life than with who won some

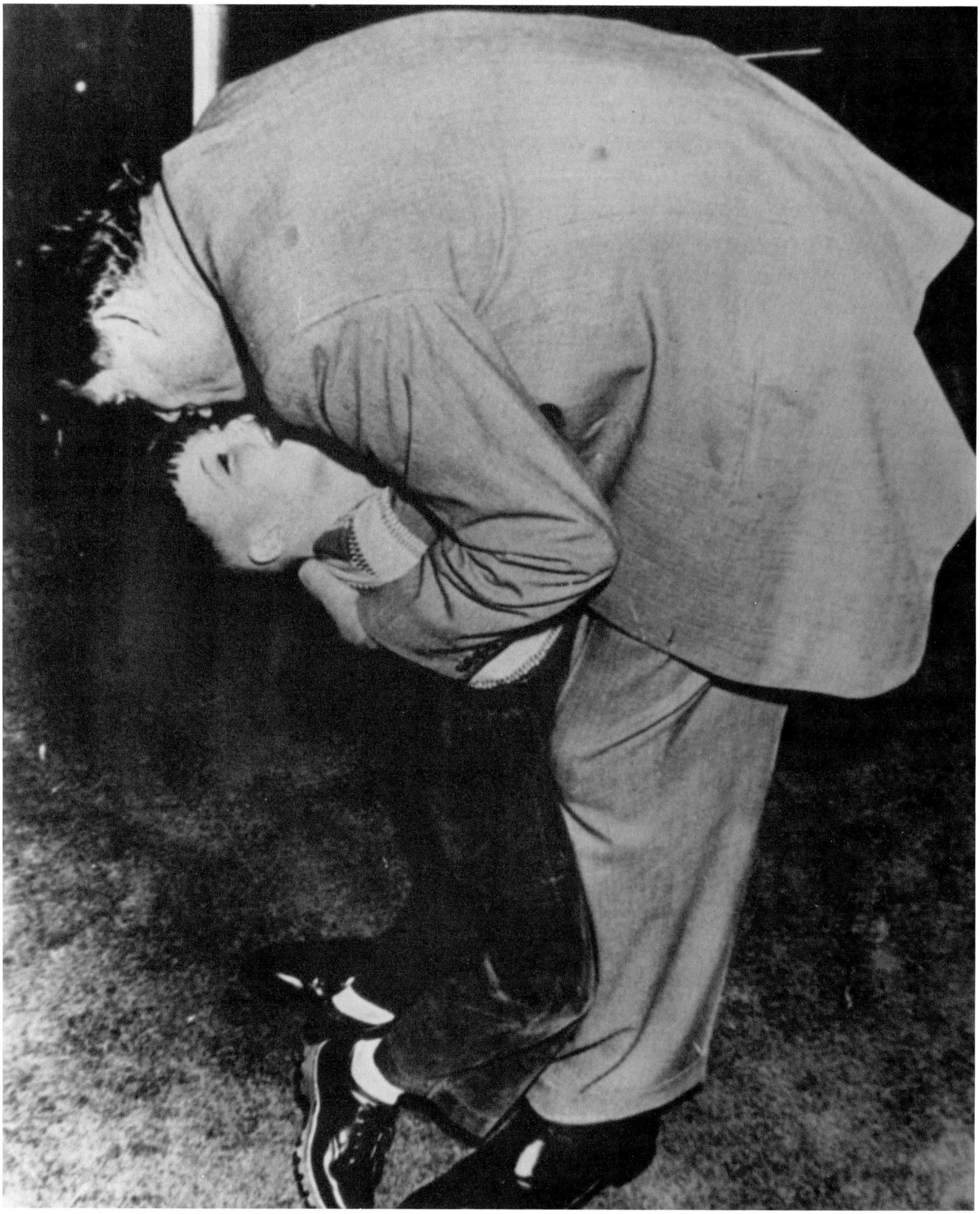

Above: John Patterson, after serving as Alabama attorney general, ran for governor in 1958 and defeated a field of Democratic contenders that included George C. Wallace who was making his first bid for office. Although Alabama Democrats voted under the symbol of a white rooster, the donkey was the recognized symbol of the National Democratic Party. Attorney and World War II hero, Patterson humorously employed that symbol at this campaign stop in Gadsden in May 1958, illustrating the lengths to which politicians had to go to attract attention in their campaigns for elected offices. (Etowah County. ADAH.)

Left: "The Little Man's Big Friend," James E. Folsom used Southern rhetoric and Populist imagery to win election as governor in 1946 and then again in 1955. As governor, Folsom supported a liberal program for state reform, but he was less adroit in handling legislators than in persuading voters. Without legislative support, his vision for the state was not fully realized. In this circa 1955 photograph, "Big Jim" Folsom hugged his five-year-old son, "Little Jim," who followed in his father's footsteps by serving as governor from 1993 to 1995. (Courtesy of the *Montgomery Advertiser*.)

George Corley Wallace campaigned at the old Barbour County Courthouse in 1958 in his first, and only unsuccessful, bid for governor. After that loss, Wallace came back to serve an unprecedented four terms as governor—1963–1967, 1971–1979, and 1983–1987. (Barbour County. Courtesy of the Hightower Photographic Committee, Clayton.)

election. They rarely have taken politics as seriously as the politicians. In truth, they have often viewed and valued political campaigns as public entertainment. Voting percentages in Alabama have always been low. After all, no person under twenty-one could vote before 1971, when the Twenty-sixth Amendment lowered the age to eighteen. No black male voted before 1868, and later, his ballot was not always counted as cast. Indeed, between 1901 and the civil rights movement of the 1960s, he was the exception if he voted at all. No woman of any age could vote until 1920, when the Nineteenth Amendment was passed. Yet few would deny the importance of politics in Alabama history. Many consider its mastery an art and regard politics as one of the South's major contributions to the American tradition.

Rosa Parks and Johnnie Carr were photographed circa 1990 riding on a Montgomery city bus in commemoration of their key roles in the Montgomery bus boycott. Rosa Parks' refusal to give up her seat on a bus to a white person in 1955 violated city ordinances mandating bus segregation. Her stand was the incident that sparked the Montgomery bus boycott and, ultimately, the civil rights movement in this country. Johnnie Carr, who later served as president of the Montgomery Improvement Association which originally had been formed to organize the boycott, was one of those who provided grassroots leadership in the boycott that lasted for thirteen months. (Montgomery County. ADAH.)

In the spring of 1963, the Southern Christian Leadership Conference targeted Birmingham's segregated businesses for mass demonstrations that were carefully planned earlier in the year. Woolworth's segregated lunch counter was the scene of sit-in demonstrations. (Jefferson County. Courtesy of the Birmingham Public Library Department of Archives and Manuscripts.)

In 1956, Autherine Lucy of Marengo County became the first African-American admitted to the University of Alabama; however, she was able to attend classes safely for only one day. Angry crowds threatened her, and, when she blamed the University's trustees for not ensuring her safety, they expelled her. Lucy's lawyers in her suit to gain admission were Thurgood Marshall (center) and Arthur Shores of Birmingham (in front). Marshall later became the first black justice on the U.S. Supreme Court. (Jefferson County. Courtesy of the William Stanley Hoole Special Collections Library, University of Alabama.)

*34*

In 1965, most African-Americans still were denied the right to vote in Alabama. African-Americans in Dallas County began protests against white voting officials in Selma in early 1965. They decided to carry their protest to the Capitol to make people aware of their struggle for voting rights. On March 7, 1965, civil rights marchers and law enforcement personnel clashed at the Edmund Pettus Bridge over the Alabama River in Selma. The conflict at the beginning of the Selma to Montgomery march became known as Bloody Sunday. The national publicity generated by the march contributed to the passage of the Voting Rights Act in August 1965, and widespread voter registration drives were organized. Today Alabama has one of the highest percentages of elected black officials of any state in the nation. (Dallas County. ADAH.)

After ratification of the Nineteenth Amendment to the U.S Constitution in 1920, Alabama women were slow moving into politics on a statewide basis. There were, however, notable exceptions. Sybil Pool of Linden served in the state legislature from 1936 to 1944, and Agnes Baggett held elected offices in state government for twenty-eight years. In 1950, Baggett resigned her position as assistant clerk of the Alabama Supreme Court to run for the office of secretary of state. Her remarkable political career included three terms as secretary of state (1951–1955, 1963–1967, and 1975–1979), one term as state auditor (1955–1959), and two terms as state treasurer (1959–1962 and 1967–1975). At a meeting circa 1968, then state treasurer Baggett sat between Governor Albert Brewer (on the left) and Reverend John Vickers of the St. James Church in Montgomery. On the wall above the group is a poster for George Wallace's 1968 bid for the presidency of the United States. Vickers was the Wallace family minister in Montgomery and had performed the funeral service for Lurleen Burns Wallace in May 1968. (Montgomery County. ADAH.)

L. A. Conoley (seated) and Thomas Morris were members of the Independent Blues of Selma. The state legislature created the Alabama Volunteer Corps (AVC) in February 1860 to encompass the many new volunteer militia companies then being formed. Companies chose their own uniforms until the AVC suggested one in March 1861. The Independent Blues uniforms conformed closely to the AVC regulation uniform. Members of the Blues wore shakos with a round, sky-blue-over-white pompon and brass cap plate; a dark blue frock coat with sky blue trim on the collar, pointed cuffs, and a single row of buttons; white or sky blue epaulets; and cadet gray pants with white stripes. The familiar Confederate gray uniform began to appear in the summer and fall of 1861; however, many of the old blue uniforms were worn well into 1862. (Dallas County. ADAH.)

# three
*Alabama's Military Heritage*

The South is often characterized as an area of intense loyalty, a region that carries its patriotism and support of country to the point of war if necessary. Alabama fits that mold, and its military heritage is an integral part of its political and social history.

As a slave state, Alabama supported the bid of Texas to win its independence from Mexico and furnished men and arms to the American cause in the Mexican War, which resulted from the United States' annexation of Texas. A martial spirit was kept alive through militia companies formed in counties and towns across the state. Militia musters were social and civic events, and being an officer in a local militia unit often was a stepping stone to a political career. These military companies took on greater significance when Alabama seceded from the Union in 1861.

Alabama is forever identified with the Confederacy. The state's secession occurred at the capitol in Montgomery, as did the formation of the Confederate States of America. Jefferson Davis stood on the portico of the Alabama State Capitol and took the oath of office as the new nation's first and only president. The state furnished the Southern government with sixty-three infantry regiments, twelve to fifteen cavalry regiments, and eighteen or more batteries of artillery. An estimated 120,000

Above: James Madison Deas served in Company "D" of the Thirty-second Alabama Infantry. This portrait of the Clarke County native was taken circa 1862 and reflects the proud fierceness and optimism of Alabama Confederates in the early part of the Civil War. (Clarke County. ADAH.)

On August 5, 1864, during the Battle of Mobile Bay, the fleet of Admiral David G. Farragut succeeded in passing the forts at the entrance of the bay and in defeating the Confederate ironclad *C.S.S. Tennessee*. From then until August 23, Fort Morgan was pounded by both naval and land-based artillery. This photograph was taken after the surrender of the fort. (Baldwin County. ADAH.)

In May 1893, Jefferson Davis' body lay in state in the Supreme Court Chamber of the Capitol building where thirty-two years earlier he had been inaugurated president of the Confederate States of America. Montgomery photographer H. P. Tresslar took a series of photographs documenting the occasion. This event occurred as the body of Davis, who died in 1889, was being transported to Richmond, Virginia, for reinterment in Hollywood Cemetery. (Montgomery County. ADAH.)

white Alabamians fought for the Confederacy, and no state contributed a greater percentage of its population to the cause. At the same time, as many as 2,500 white Alabamians, mainly from hill counties such as Winston and Walker, fought for the Union. Black Alabamians contributed to the war effort on both sides. Some 10,000 enlisted and served with Northern regiments during Federal occupation of North Alabama, and, on the Confederate side, slaves often went to military camps with their owners or were hired or rented to built defensive works and railroads. Alabama also contributed food and military supplies, especially from the extensive manufacturing works in Selma.

From foot soldiers to thirty-six generals, from heroes such as Major John H. Pelham, whom General Robert E. Lee called "gallant," to Admiral Raphael Semmes, who commanded the C.S.S. *Alabama*, Confederate Alabamians fought bravely and against

The Bessemer Rifles, photographed at Camp O'Neal in 1891, was typical of the local companies which formed the Alabama state troops. In 1897, these units were designated as the Alabama National Guard. The man standing fourth from the left is Thomas M. Owen, first director of the Alabama Archives. (ADAH.)

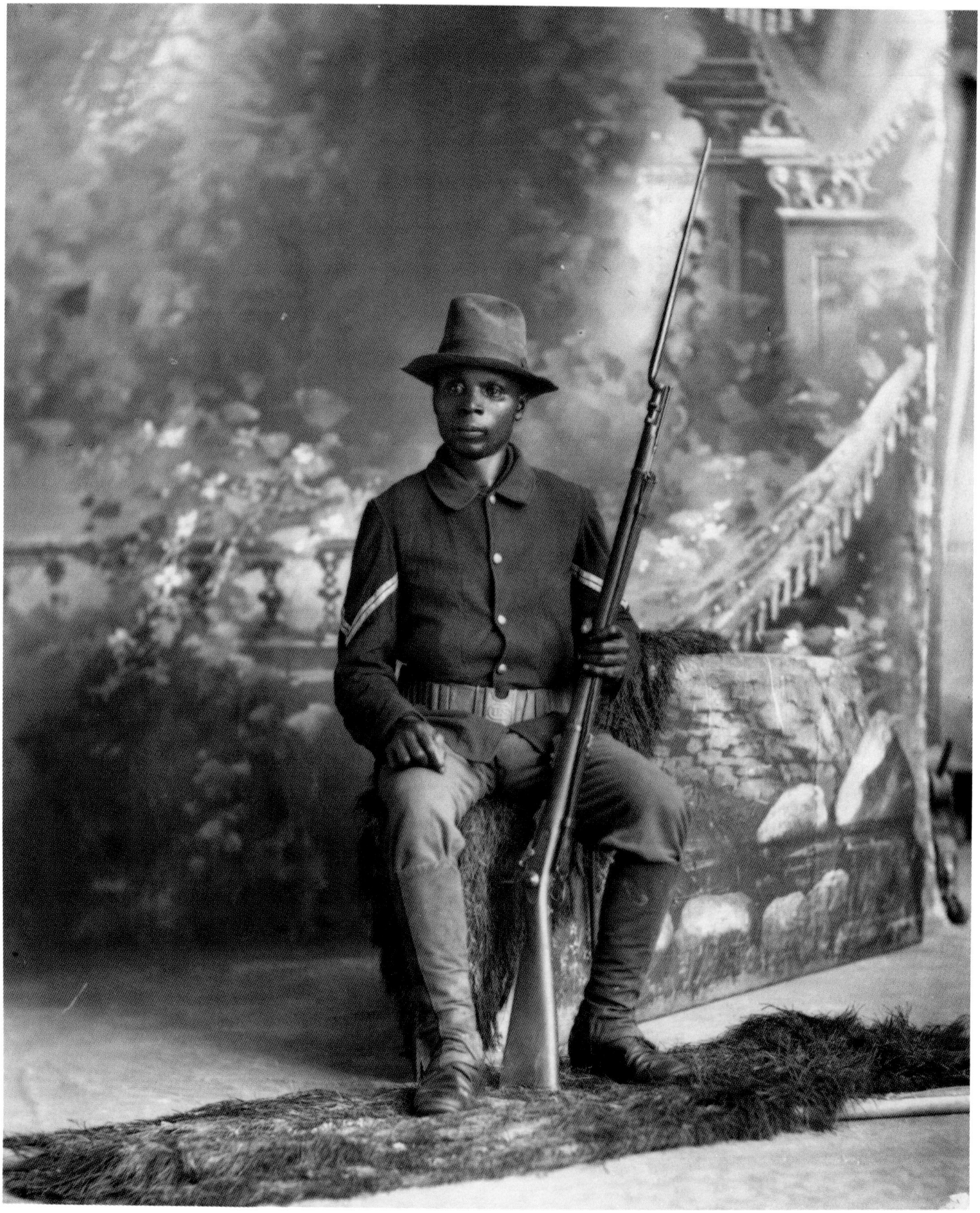

Edmund Winchester Rucker lost his left arm during the Civil War. He later was a successful Birmingham businessman and active in Confederate veterans groups. Children growing up in Alabama in the late nineteenth and early twentieth centuries have vivid memories of the large number of men with peg legs or empty sleeves. (Jefferson County. ADAH.)

Left: In 1898, Corporal M. W. Parlee was a member of the Third Alabama. As with most state troops, black and white, Parlee was not armed with the new Krag–Jorgensen bolt-action rifle that was issued to regular units. (Mobile County. Courtesy of the University of South Alabama Archives.)

Alabamians of African descent fought on both sides in the Civil War. Thousands enlisted in the Union Army during Federal occupation of North Alabama. Slaves often accompanied their masters to Confederate military camps and into battle or were hired for military construction projects. In 1931, several African-Americans who had seen Confederate service attended the Confederate Veterans Reunion in Montgomery. Pictured left to right are Steve Manuel, age eighty-two, of Marks, Mississippi; Ed Byrd of Charlotte, North Carolina; William Wilson, age eighty, of Standle, North Carolina; Samuel and Delila Martin, age eighty-one and seventy-seven respectively, of Mansfield, Arkansas; and William Gaskin, age eighty-four, of Lowndes County, Alabama. (Montgomery County. ADAH.)

On May 12, 1909, veterans of the Fourth Ohio Cavalry returned the battle flag of the Rifle Scouts to Alabama at the state convention of the United Daughters of the Confederacy in Huntsville. Union troops had captured the flag during the Battle of Selma in April 1865. Seated in the center of the group was Virginia Tunstall Clay Clopton. Mrs. Clopton's first husband was C. C. Clay Jr. who served as one of Alabama's U. S. senators in 1861. When Alabama seceded, Clay and his Senate colleague, Benjamin Fitzpatrick, resigned their seats. (Madison County. ADAH.)

General Joseph "Fighting Joe" Wheeler sat astride the horse presented to him in Huntsville during the Spanish-American War. Wheeler, a lieutenant general in the Confederate Army at age twenty-eight and an Alabama congressman during the 1880s and 1890s, was commissioned major general of volunteers during the Spanish-American War. (Madison County. ADAH.)

heavy odds. During the four years of fighting, approximately 40,000 Alabamians died and another 35,000 were disabled.

Alabamians fought on native soil and on battlefields across the South and beyond it. At Gettysburg alone the state's losses were 1,750 men killed and hundreds of others captured or wounded. Within the state, the Tennessee Valley was the site of much military activity, and the Battle of Mobile Bay on August 5, 1864, is one of the nation's most heralded naval engagements. In the spring of 1865, General James H. Wilson led a destructive cavalry raid through Alabama that resulted in Union victory at the Battle of Selma on April 2, 1865, and the surrender of Montgomery on April 12. In a final touch of irony, the state where the Confederate States of America was born became the scene of the last Confederate surrender east of the Mississippi River. On May 4, 1865, Major General Richard Taylor surrendered his troops to General E. R. S. Canby at Citronelle.

After Reconstruction, Alabama returned to the old pattern of having military companies and a state militia. When the Spanish-American War broke out in 1898, President William McKinley assigned quotas to the states. Alabama furnished three regiments of infantry. The First Alabama was commanded by Col. E. L. Higdon, the Second by Col. J. W. Cox, and the Third (a black regiment) by Col. R. L. Bullard.

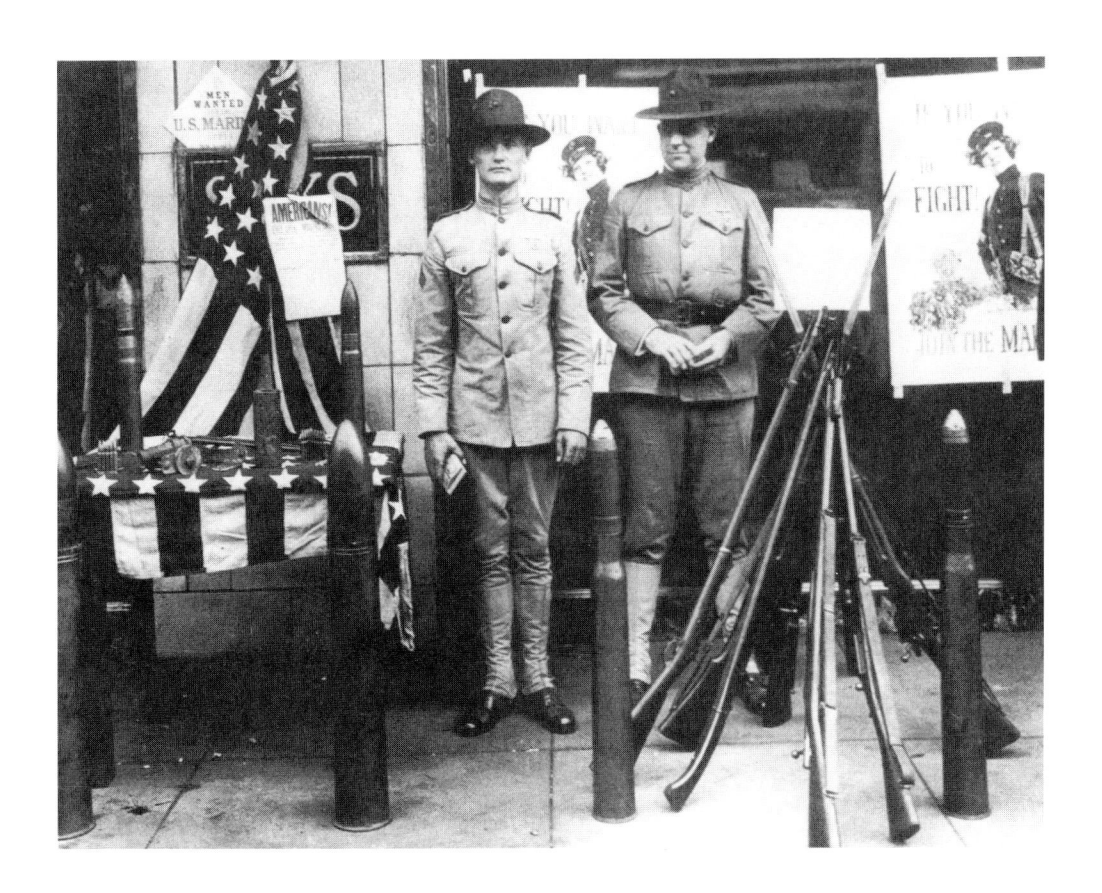

Two Alabamians gained national prominence during the Spanish-American War. Joseph S. Wheeler, already famous as a twenty-eight-year-old cavalry lieutenant general in the Civil War, was commissioned major general of volunteers and once again demonstrated his military skills. Richard Pearson Hobson became a national hero with his daring, but unsuccessful, efforts to sink the collier *Merrimac* in the channel of Santiago harbor and bottle up the Spanish squadron.

When the United States entered World War I in 1917, Alabamians, with few exceptions, rallied behind the president and manifested their traditional patriotism. Alabama's "Fighting Fourth" Regiment was recalled from the Mexican border where it was trying to catch Pancho Villa. The regiment was sent

In 1917, America entered World War I on the side of the Allies—France, Russia, Britain, and Italy—who had been fighting against Germany and the Austro-Hungarian Empire since 1914. Americans worked quickly to prepare for war. Almost 100,000 men in Alabama enlisted or were drafted to serve in the Army, Navy, or Marines. (Jefferson County. Courtesy of the Birmingham Public Library Department of Archives and Manuscripts.)

Among those eager to join the military and fight the enemy were these conscripted men from Evergreen. They were on their way to Mobile and then, they hoped, to Berlin to relay the fervent, if misspelled, sentiments written on the side of their railroad car—"To Hell Mit the Keiser." (Conecuh County. ADAH.)

William Dumas was a farmer in Wilcox County when he enlisted or was drafted into the Army during World War I. Dumas, whose father had been born into slavery in 1856, was educated at Camden Academy, belonged to the Grand United Order of Odd Fellows of America, and was a member of the Missionary Baptist Church. Private Dumas, married and with one child, reported to Camp McClellan in August 1918 and died in camp on October 25, 1918, possibly from the influenza epidemic that swept the country in that year. (Wilcox County. ADAH.)

Left: On the home front, women looked for ways to serve the war effort. During World War I that sometimes meant serving in the Motor Corps Staff of the National League for Woman's Service. In Montgomery, Sergeant Mrs. Sidney Winter (driving) and Sergeant Mrs. J. M. Anderson drove Major Manoher and Colonel Stanson of division headquarters across camp on official business. (Montgomery County. ADAH.)

Henry A. Onderdonk of Rutan left Chatom High School to join the Army when the United States entered World War I. He enlisted in Mobile and eventually was assigned to the 167th Regiment of the famed Rainbow Division. This photograph was taken during his sister's visit to Camp Mills in New York. First Private Onderdonk was killed in action in France on July 27, 1918. He is buried in grave No. 87 at the French Military Cemetery at Chateau Thierry. (Washington County. ADAH.)

45

In May 1919, Alabama's 167th Regiment of the famed Rainbow Division came home to Birmingham and was welcomed by thousands of cheering citizens. This photograph was taken on Birmingham's Twentieth Street. After their welcome in Birmingham, the 167th traveled to Montgomery where the men were mustered out of service on May 12. (Jefferson County. Courtesy of the Birmingham Public Library Department of Archives and Manusctipts.)

to France as part of the 167th Infantry, which in turn became a part of the Forty-second "Rainbow" Division. Alabama furnished about 95,000 troops, 74,000 of whom were drafted. In France, Alabama soldiers took part in the bloody engagements at Chateau-Thierry, St. Mihiel Salient, and the Argonne Forest. In all, 2,401 Alabamians were killed in action, and 3,861 died from wounds or disease.

When the armistice ending the war was signed on November 11, 1918, the Birmingham *Age-Herald* declared it was "the greatest day in history," marking "the beginning of a new era for humanity." However, the peace was not long lived. New military alliances and separate acts of aggression by the Axis powers resulted in World War II. During that global conflict in the 1940s, Alabama became a significant part of the nation's engine of total war.

Alabamians, numbering 250,000, served in the armed forces, and approximately 6,000 gave their lives. Military posts at Maxwell Field, Gunter Field, Craig Field, Camp McClellan, Brookley Field, and Camp Rucker trained pilots, women soldiers, and other military personnel on a large scale. At Tuskegee the nation's first black aviation cadets were trained and formed into the Ninety-ninth Pursuit Squadron. The pilots distinguished themselves in

The Alabama National Guard provided security and crowd control during the Scottsboro Boys Trial in Jackson County in 1931. The trail, in which nine young African-American men were falsely accused of raping two white women, has been cited as dramatic testimony about how racial problems were intensified by the economic problems of the Depression. (Jackson County. ADAH.)

In 1924, aircraft mechanics posed with a Martin bomber, the first multiengine aircraft assigned to Maxwell Field in Montgomery. The group of mechanics represented the total Army Air Service's aircraft mechanics in the southeastern United States since there were no active bases south of Langley Field in Virginia and east of the Mississippi River. Sergeant James O. Foster, crew chief, sat in front of the right wheel. (Montgomery County. ADAH.)

Local United Service Organizations (USO) clubs held dances and parties to entertain the troops stationed in their town. This young couple competed in a jitterbug contest at a formal USO dance at Maxwell Field in Montgomery. (Montgomery County. ADAH.)

During World War II, many Alabama cities were home to military installations. The Soldiers Center Association and servicemen's clubs like this one in Mobile provided homes away from home for the soldiers and sailors stationed in the area. In addition to providing "clean" and "dry" places for the soldiers, they offered a variety of entertainment, often hosted by local citizens. (Mobile County. Courtesy of the University of South Alabama Archives.)

The Fourth Aviation Squadron sponsored a formal dance in September 1942 to show its appreciation to the members of the Girls Service Organization who had made them feel so welcome during their time in Montgomery. This USO Club for African-American soldiers was located at 215 Monroe Street in Montgomery. (Montgomery County. ADAH.)

Herbert Carter, on the right, was a member of the Ninety-ninth Pursuit Squadron, the first black fighter squadron in the U. S. Army. The Ninety-ninth trained at the Tuskegee Army Air Field and flew missions in North Africa, Sicily, Italy, Germany, Austria, and the Balkans. (Macon County. Courtesy of Herbert Carter.)

Italy, and their ranks produced two future Air Force generals, Benjamin O. Davis Jr. and Daniel "Chappie" James. War came close to home as German U-boats operated in Gulf waters off Mobile and 15,000 prisoners of war were incarcerated in camps across the state.

World War II was the catalyst for many changes in Alabama. The civilian population, men and women, worked in war plants and at shipyards as wartime spending helped promote the state's economic improvement and effectively ended the Great Depression. Higher salaries improved living conditions for blacks and poor whites, and women

Colonel Elmer Bolling, U. S. Army Air Corps, was commander of Maxwell Field when he reviewed a squadron of the Women's Army Corps during World War II. (Montgomery County. ADAH.)

49

Entertainment and patriotism were harnessed to help finance World War II. War bond drives such as this one in Mobile were common scenes across Alabama. (Mobile County. Courtesy of the University of South Alabama Archives.)

Five hundred German prisoners of war from Rommel's Afrika Korps were escorted from the Aliceville train depot to the POW camp on June 2, 1943. The Aliceville camp was erected in 1942 and had four hundred frame barracks which could house 6,000 prisoners, as well as American military personnel. By mid-September, 5,300 German soldiers and 1,029 American personnel lived at the Aliceville camp. Because of labor shortages created by the war, the POWs worked outside the camp in Aliceville and in other areas of the state on projects ranging from timber cutting to peanut harvesting.
Most of the prisoners spent their days working to improve conditions in the camp. They built a greenhouse and planted gardens in the camp. They replaced wooden trenches built by Americans with ones made of brick the prisoners molded and baked themselves. They constructed a 1,000-seat amphitheater where the camp 40-member orchestra performed. The prisoners also organized six small bands, glee clubs, a dance orchestra, a string quartet, and a 25-member choir for church services. The acting guild presented plays, and the prisoners purchased a printing press to publish a camp newspaper, *Der Zaungast (The Guest Inside the Wire)*. By 1945, all of the prisoners were transferred from Aliceville to other camps in the United States and then, after the war ended, returned to Germany. (Pickens County. ADAH.)

Above: With the labor shortage created by World War II, old prejudices about women in the work place were put aside—even if only temporarily. Mobile, with its large shipbuilding industry and airplane repair and supply depot at Brookley Field, actively recruited women to fill the thousands of jobs created by the war effort. By 1944, women constituted 10 percent of employees in the shipyards and almost half of the work force in Alabama airplane and ordnance plants. With the war's end, however, work opportunities declined. By 1950, employment of women on a statewide level was only slightly higher than it had been in 1940. These women worked as welders for the Alabama Dry Dock and Shipbuilding Company during World War II. (Mobile County. Courtesy of the University of South Alabama Archives.)

During World War II, patriots on the home front mounted efforts to support the troops. The American Legion Auxiliary sponsored this waste paper drive at a salvage depot in Florence. (Lauderdale County. ADAH.)

Right: One million six hundred thousand Americans served in the armed forces during the Korean War. In February 1951, First Lieutenant Will Hill Tankersley, like thousands of other servicemen, recorded his experience in a photograph sent to his family back home in Montgomery. Lieutenant Tankersley, a West Point graduate, was a member of the Second Platoon Heavy Mortar Company, Nineteenth Infantry Regiment, Twenty-Fourth Infantry Division of the U.S. Army. (Korea. Courtesy of Will Hill Tankersley.)

During the Korean and Vietnam Wars, Alabama again played a major military role. Many U.S. Army helicopter pilots were trained at Ft. Rucker in Ozark. The TH-55 "Osage" was used as a primary helicopter trainer at Ft. Rucker from 1965 to 1988. (Dale County. Courtesy of the U. S. Army Aviation Museum.)

took a more prominent role in the work force. Families moved from farms and rural areas to cities. New educational opportunities, especially those funded by the GI bill, and the chance to own homes with mortgages secured by federal programs moved many Alabama families into the middle class. The war helped transform Alabama, causing sweeping changes in the lives of its citizens.

As in past conflicts, Alabamians answered the call of their country during the Korean War of the 1950s, the Vietnam War of the next decade, and the Gulf War and other military actions in the 1990s. The military spirit of Alabama—born of its frontier experience, out-of-doors lifestyle, sense of honor, love of country, and, according to some historians, its warlike Celtic heritage—is woven through the state's history from generation to succeeding generation.

The riverboat *City of Knoxville* sat at the dock before being loaded in Decatur in the 1880s. (Morgan County. ADAH.)

# four
## *Agriculture*

Politics and military conflicts helped to shape Alabama; however, it is impossible to understand the state without understanding the fact that Alabama was a rural, agricultural state from its territorial beginning through the first half of the twentieth century. As late as 1940, 70 percent of the population was still rural. For most of its history, agriculture was the main source of employment and income for the people of Alabama.

The majority of Alabamians who depended upon the land for their livelihood were yeoman farmers. Before 1865, only a scattering of these small independent farmers owned any slaves. These self-sufficient men and women lived in the hill countries in the north, the Wiregrass region of the southeast, the piney woods in the southwest, as well as in the Black Belt and Tennessee Valley. They cultivated cotton, planted corn and grains, worked vegetable gardens, and raised chickens, hogs, and cattle for home consumption. Their farms were modest in size, but they owned their land and performed their own labor.

Early in the state's history, cotton was the major money crop. Although cultivation was general, cotton planting became concentrated in the rich lands of central Alabama's Black Belt counties and

Above: Until the early part of the twentieth century, late summers in Alabama were much the same as they had been before the Civil War. Men, women, and children went into the fields to pick cotton. (Courtesy of the Birmingham Public Library Department of Archives and Manuscripts.)

the alluvial soil of the Tennessee Valley in North Alabama. Encouraged by generally high cotton prices and generous returns on their investments, planters in these areas increased their acreage and built comfortable houses. Cotton was king, and because of this prosperity from the sale of cotton, antebellum Alabama became one of the wealthiest and most rapidly growing parts of the nation.

The men, and sometimes women, who owned the larger plantations were dependent upon slave labor, and slavery became an integral part of the plantation economy. The plantation-slavery system produced a broadcloth aristocracy that dominated the state's antebellum social and economic life and strongly influenced, although it did not control, the state's government. Only 6.4 percent of the state's white population owned slaves in 1860, but probably one-third of Alabama families included a slaveholder. Slaves, numbering 435,080, made up 45.48 percent of the state's total population of over 900,000. Another 2,690 "free persons of color" lived in the state in 1860.

Although the Civil War destroyed slavery and the Thirteenth Amendment made its prohibition perpetual, many planters retained their status in the community and emerged from the Reconstruction

The Martin Dallas Waldrop homestead located on the Etowah-DeKalb County line was a typical mid-nineteenth-century farm with well house, shingled roof, and split rail fence. (Etowah–DeKalb Counties. Courtesy of Eloise McClendon.)

The Tennessee Valley was an important cotton producing region. Farmers would haul their ginned and baled cotton to the local market for purchase by cotton brokers. Streets in Huntsville circa 1900 often were clogged with bales of cotton. (Madison County. Postcard from the collections of the ADAH.)

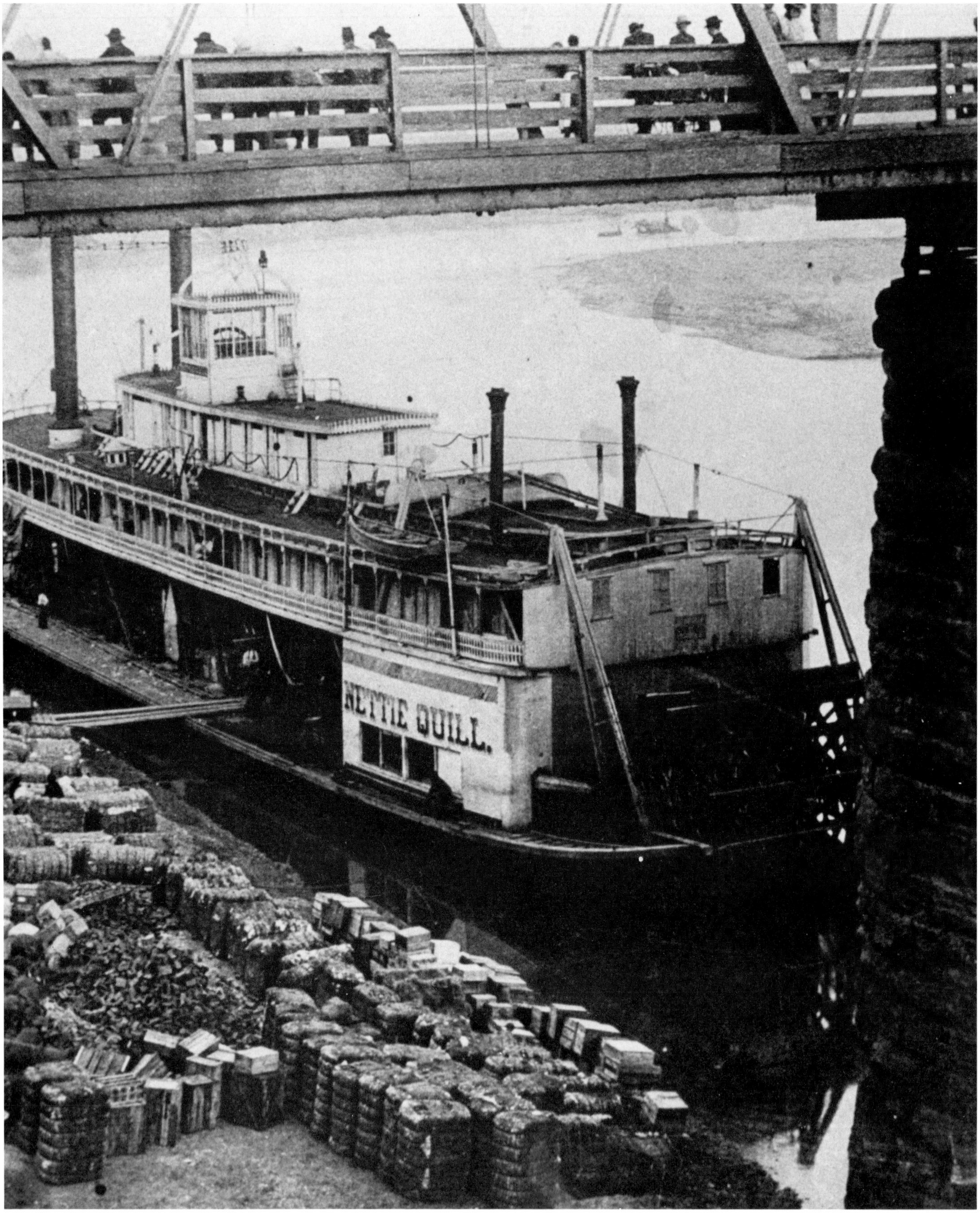
NETTIE QUILL.

Eufaula was an important cotton shipping town. In this photograph taken around 1910, cotton bales were stacked on North Randolph Street ready for shipment. (Barbour County. Courtesy of Doug Purcell.)

Left: The steamboat *Nettie Quill* waited at the dock in Selma circa 1900 to be loaded with cotton for shipment down river to Mobile. (Dallas County. Courtesy of the Old Depot Museum.)

era still in possession of most of their lands. With the system of slave labor abolished, landowners developed new arrangements to secure and maintain dependable labor, and cotton remained the primary commercial crop. Through the tenant farmer and crop lien systems, most former slaves and a substantial number of whites worked the land. There were many variations, but generally a landowner made a contract with the laborer to farm land. Instead of paying rent in money, the tenant paid with his labor. He divided the returns from the harvested crop with the owner, paid off his loans, and kept what was left over.

Most tenants also signed mortgages or liens on the crop with nearby crossroads merchants in return for food and farm supplies to be picked up as needed. The tenant was to pay his bill to the merchant out of the crop money that he divided with the landowner. Unfortunately, as volume

This is reputedly the first photograph taken of the first cotton picking machine. Lucy Belle Railey took it in 1908 near Selma with a Brownie Kodak camera and sent copies to the inventors and owners. (Dallas County. ADAH.)

57

Photographed about 1915, these Autauga County cotton planters—J. W. Oliver, Howard Doster, John Wadsworth, Jack Taylor, and John Alexander—stopped at a local store after attending an agricultural meeting. The photograph, titled Big Cotton Planters, may have referred to more than their land holdings or cotton production. Steeped in traditional ways, many planters were suspicious of the advice of scientific book farmers from the land-grant colleges at Auburn, Tuskegee Institute, and Alabama A & M in Huntsville. (Autauga County. Courtesy of the Auburn University Archives.)

Although much of the agricultural labor, both white and black, was controlled through a tenant farming or sharecrop system, some Alabama farmers managed to maintain their land and their independence. The average white Alabama sharecropper earned about $14 an acre in good times and $8 when times were hard. A black sharecropper earned even less. Despite urging from agricultural specialists at Auburn and Tuskegee Institute which had excellent agricultural extension programs, Alabama farmers—from the big planters to sharecroppers—were reluctant to diversify their crops. This photograph was taken circa 1900. (Macon County. Courtesy of Tuskegee University Archives.)

Alabama farmers relied upon the services of cotton gins that separated cotton seeds from the fiber. In 1927, local farmers hauled their picked cotton to the gin at Mt. Hope. (Lawrence County. ADAH.)

production rose without a matching increase in demand by the market, cotton prices decreased, and, as often as not, the sharecropper did not make a profit and frequently could not pay his bills. The situation became a hopeless cycle of spiraling debt as the tenant worked the next year to pay off the previous year's obligations. The tenant farmer–crop lien system developed as a temporary expedient; however, it became a continuous curse and a form of bondage.

Poverty in the post–Civil War decades wore down individuals, families, and social institutions. Increasingly, small farmers, no longer able to afford traditional self-sufficient production modes, switched to market farming, took jobs in local towns or nearby plants, or left the farm altogether. They and their families made personal sacrifices, hoping that by practicing strict economy the burden of debt could be eased.

World War I brought a brief upturn in agriculture, but a sharp decline followed again in the 1920s and further disaster came with the Great Depression. By the 1930s, Alabama and the South had become what President Franklin D. Roosevelt called the "nation's number-one economic problem." Roosevelt's New Deal agricultural program, carried

By the early 1900s, the boll weevil was moving rapidly across the South from Texas, ravishing cotton crops as it went and forcing farmers to diversify. Profits from peanuts, sweet potatoes, sugar cane, hogs, and vegetables proved greater than profits from cotton. In 1918, the city of Enterprise erected a statue honoring the boll weevil "in profound appreciation" for the prosperity the insect brought to Coffee County by forcing farmers to move to other crops. (Coffee County. Courtesy of the Auburn University Archives.)

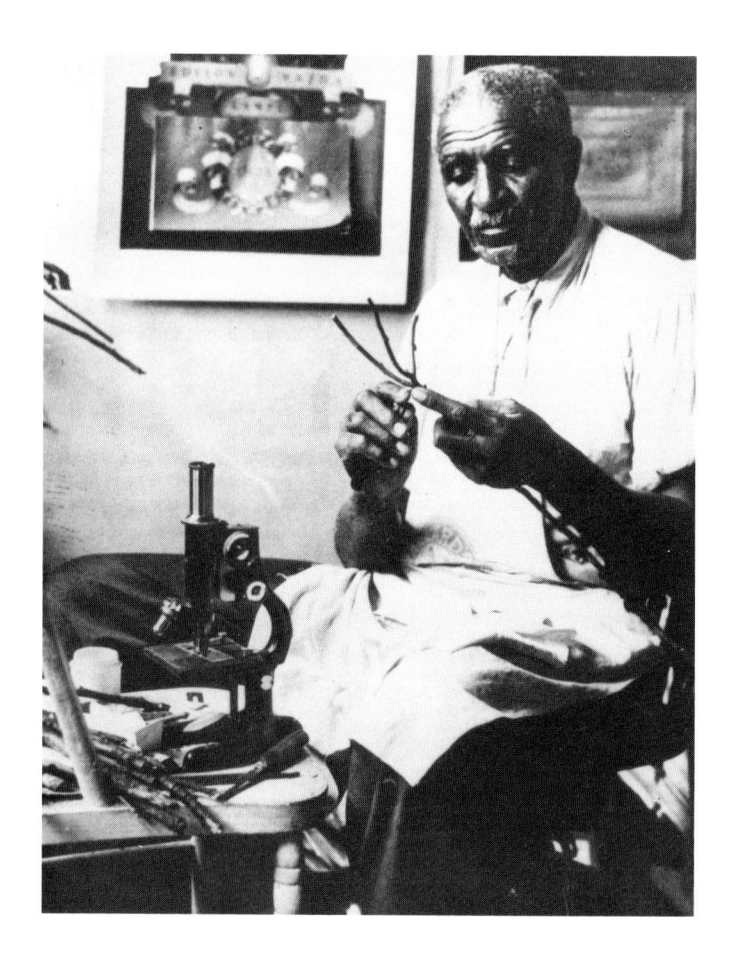

In the Wiregrass, peanuts became the most important crop, fostering peanut festivals, peanut bowls, and the naming of peanut queens. (Houston County. Courtesy of the Houston Love Memorial Library.)

Right: Dr. George Washington Carver, a scientist at Tuskegee Institute, gained national recognition for his research on uses for peanuts, sweet potatoes, cotton, and pecans. Among his other scientific and agricultural work, Dr. Carver studied diseases of Southern plants. He contributed hundreds of rare specimens to the Division of Mycology of the U.S. Department of Agriculture. (Macon County. ADAH.)

60

Mr. T. A. Whatley, an Opelika farmer, literally reaped the benefits of crop diversification. Whatley was photographed in the 1930s with the twenty-seven different products grown on his farm. (Lee County. ADAH.)

Radio technology softened the isolation of rural Alabamians and enabled county agents to communicate information to farmers more efficiently. Before individual families could afford their own radios, people would gather in schools or at the county courthouse to hear special programs. On February 4, 1926, home demonstration agent Thalia Bell held a lantern while the East View ladies home demonstration club listened to a broadcast at Sandy Creek.
(Tallapoosa County. Courtesy of the Auburn University Archives.)

County agents were charged with improving the quality of rural life in Alabama, as well as with increasing the cash income of farmers. M. A. Barnes from the Cooperative Extension Service installed a system to move water from the Rickard family's outside well to a faucet in the kitchen. The cost circa 1928 was $27.00. (Franklin County. Courtesy of the Auburn University Archives.)

out in large part under the Agricultural Adjustment Act, served large and medium farmers. For the vast numbers of black and white sharecroppers and their families, there was only limited assistance.

Beginning in the 1910s, the destruction wrought by the boll weevil on Alabama cotton forced farmers to experiment with new crops. Henry, Dale, Coffee, Houston, and other southeast Wiregrass counties benefited from switching to peanut production. The lowly goober revived an entire section of the state. George Washington Carver, the internationally recognized black scientist at Tuskegee Institute, developed new products from peanuts and demonstrated the potential value of other vegetables such as sweet potatoes.

Beginning at the turn of the century refrigerated railroad cars made possible the shipment of perishable vegetables and fruits, and truck farming became important. Experiments conducted at Auburn, Alabama's land-grant college, and federal programs made possible by the Smith-Lever Act of 1914 and other laws also helped the farmer. Selective breeding strengthened livestock, soybeans became a money crop, and improved strains of seeds, particularly hybrid corn, were developed. The state's timber, which had been destructively clear-cut by loggers, made a dramatic comeback through reforestation.

World War II produced another period of prosperity for the state's farmers, but recession set in again after 1945. However, its effects were less severe and of shorter duration than the Great Depression because the number of farmers and the state's dependence on agriculture had declined. The most significant change in agriculture after World War II was mechanization. Tractors replaced mules, and farm machinery became more sophisticated and more costly. Farming evolved into a highly

Representatives of the Alabama Cooperative Extension Service gave classes in food preparation and canning to homemakers. A home demonstration agent showed proper canning methods to a group at the Frank Taylor home. (Montgomery County. Courtesy of the Auburn University Archives.)

Occupational classes were available to farmers and young men to teach them how to make the most of the resources available to them. This farm mechanics class, circa 1930s, displayed repaired and rebuilt farm equipment. (Marion County. ADAH.)

Curb markets allowed local farmers to sell their produce and town residents to purchase fresh vegetables and farm produce. The cash income was important to farmers, and curb markets provided them an important option for marketing their crops. (Etowah County. Courtesy of the Auburn University Archives.)

Turkeys became an important cash crop for Alabama farmers. In 1927, Andrew Granville DeSherbinin, one of the first farmers to turn to turkey production, raised one thousand turkeys. With his son and daughter, he loaded the birds on a wagon that Dan Walker delivered to Farm Bureau representative and marketing specialist, J. D. Moore, for a cooperative turkey sale. (Dallas County. Courtesy of the Auburn University Archives.)

Small farmers relied on dairy cows and beef cattle for products for home consumption. In May 1939, Mrs. Watkins milked one of her cows on her farm in Coffee County. (Coffee County. ADAH.)

The culmination of the agricultural year always was the county fair, such as this one in Tallapoosa County. Produce, farm animals, quilts, jellies, jams, and cakes were judged for excellence. The goal of farm families was to win as many ribbons—preferably blue ones—as possible. (Tallapoosa County. Courtesy of the Auburn University Archives.)

Mechanization of cotton production was slow and expensive, but by the 1920s larger farms were using tractors instead of mule power. After World War II, the rate of mechanism increased dramatically. For example, by 1960 almost all cotton was picked by machines. In 1937, this farmer used a disc plow to turn under his pea cover crop for fertilizer. The next year's crop would be corn and cotton. (Butler County. ADAH.)

Kudzu was brought into Alabama to protect farmland against erosion and to provide feed for farm animals. Kudzu was first introduced into the United States at the Japanese Pavilion at the Philadelphia Centennial Exposition in 1876. It was valued as a shade plant because of its dense foliage. From about 1910 to 1935, it also was cultivated as livestock pasturage, fodder, and hay. In 1935, the Alabama Agricultural Experiment Station at Auburn recommended kudzu to control soil erosion and began a massive planting campaign in the state. Today the rapidly growing vine almost has taken over the state and become the subject of numerous jokes. This photograph was taken circa 1940. (Calhoun County. Courtesy of the Auburn University Archives.)

This photograph from the files of the Farm Security Administration provides stark testimony to the toll of erosion on Alabama farm lands in the 1930s. The county is not known, but it could have been any one of dozens of Alabama counties. (Courtesy of the Library of Congress.)

Colonel Price C. McLemore invented the "Sizz Weeder," then said to be the greatest farm invention since Cyrus McCormick's reaper and Eli Whitney's cotton gin. Its purpose was to kill the weeds around cotton plants without hoeing or using herbicides. This photograph of the 1946 model of the flame cultivator was made at "The Oaks," McLemore's farm, in November 1945. (Montgomery County. ADAH.)

specialized commercial operation—commonly referred to today as agribusiness.

In the last half of the twentieth century, Alabama's farm population declined dramatically, and, by 1990, stood at 85,000, slightly more than 2 percent in a state of 4 million people. Although farm acreage and the number of farmers fell, total farm output expanded throughout the century because of increased productivity. Agriculture remains a substantial element in the state's overall economy.

Although Alabama has become urbanized and industrialized, it is still rural in many ways. Its agrarian heritage lives on, affecting the lives and attitudes of its citizens. The ownership of land remains important, and Alabamians often have kept a close tie to the homeplace. A sense of rural heritage, a close feeling of community, an uneasiness over change, a distrust of big-city influences, and a sense of individual responsibility remain strong and defining traits of the state's personality.

Survivors of the Battle of Shiloh enjoyed a Sixty-third Anniversary Reunion on the Cincinnati riverboat *Tennessee Belle* on the Tennessee River at Muscle Shoals in 1925. (Colbert County. ADAH.)

# five
*Transportation*

Alabama's river system, much of it navigable, contributed to the expansion of the cotton kingdom. Rivers formed highways for hinterland farmers and planters and for cities and towns located on or near their banks—Selma, Tuscaloosa, Eufaula, Wetumpka, Montgomery, Guntersville, Demopolis, and Florence among them.

From the mountains the Tennessee River flows through a wide valley toward the Mississippi River; and from the hill country the Black Warrior and Tombigbee roll south to meet the Alabama. In the central part of the state the Coosa and Tallapoosa join at Wetumpka to form the Alabama, which then winds its way across the state, meeting the Tombigbee and forming the Mobile River, and flowing on into Mobile Bay. In eastern Alabama, the Chattahoochee flows out of Georgia north of Phenix City to create the Alabama-Georgia boundary and courses south to Apalachicola Bay in Florida. By the late 1820s, steamboats, both stern-wheelers and the more popular and practical side-wheeler, traveled these rivers, transporting manufactured goods upstream and returning with their decks loaded with cotton, naval stores, hides, and other agricultural produce.

The white limestone cliffs give the Tombigbee River at Demopolis a distinctive quality. For many years the only way to cross the river was by ferry. (Marengo County. Courtesy of Joe C. P. Turner and the Marengo County Historical Society.)

In 1906, the family of M. L. Vickers, ferryman on the Tallapoosa River near Horseshoe Bend Battleground, posed for a group picture. In the early nineteenth century, ferry operators were exempt from militia service. (Tallapoosa County. Courtesy of Judge C. J. Coley.)

This train, stopped at the south end of the Florence bridge over the Tennessee River, was photographed circa 1890 by Turner and Son, photographers in Florence and Gadsden. They offered "Over 100 Views for sale of this section of North Alabama, viz. Aqueduct, and other scenes on Muscle Shoals Canal, Bailey Springs, Sheffield, &C." (Lauderdale County. ADAH.)

By the turn of the century, the capacity of riverboats was increased by the use of barges. The building of Lock 17 on the Black Warrior River in 1914 opened commercial navigation all the way to Birmingham. The river became particularly important for shipping coal. (Tuscaloosa County. Courtesy of the Birmingham Public Library Department of Archives and Manuscripts.)

The first passenger train ran on the Abbeville Southern Railway on November 27, 1893. The man in the cab was George Weatherford. The locomotive was a "Grant," built in the mid-1870s and, in all probability, was the No "1" of the Alabama Midland Railway which furnished the motive power for the Abbeville Southern. (Henry County. ADAH.)

By the early 1880s, Montgomery had become a thriving railroad center with at least six rail lines serving the city. By 1894, forty-four passenger trains made scheduled stops daily. Montgomery's train station was a small, two-story antebellum frame building, captured in this stereograph circa 1887. It could hardly accommodate travelers and their friends who came to offer welcome or farewell, and passengers complained about the lack of covered walkways from tracks to the station. In 1896, the L & N Railroad let bids for the construction of the Montgomery Union Station and train shed which was completed in 1897. (Montgomery County. ADAH.)

In rural areas of Alabama, ferries often served both trains and wagons. This ferry in Elmore County provided transportation across the Tallapoosa River in 1898 for a local logging train. (Elmore County. ADAH.)

Before 1830 the state relied on its river system and inadequate dirt roads. The first railroad company was chartered by the legislature in 1830, and its two-mile line, providing transportation around part of the Muscle Shoals at Tuscumbia, was completed in 1832. The state's second railway, the Montgomery Railroad Company, was chartered in 1832 and financed by planters. These early efforts were unsuccessful, so in 1840 Charles T. Pollard obtained a loan from the state legislature and began construction of his Montgomery-West Point line. In general, however, the state was reluctant to approve funds for railroads, and the Mobile and Ohio was constructed in the 1850s largely with private capital. By 1860 the state had 743 miles of railroads, but there was no linkage between North and South Alabama, between the Tennessee and Alabama Rivers. Alabama's business remained agriculture, and its towns and cities drew their wealth from commerce instead of industry.

The Civil War proved the necessity of rail transportation, especially the need for railroads connecting North and South Alabama. During Reconstruction, Northerners and native sons gambled and invested private fortunes and public bond funds in railroad construction. Major changes

At the end of the railroad, oxen (and later mules) moved heavy loads. In 1907, equipment for gold mining operations in Tallapoosa County was transported by six yoke of oxen. (Tallapoosa County. Courtesy of Judge C. J. Coley.)

For decades, Birmingham's Terminal Station was a point of arrival and departure for visitors and residents. The road under the station and the tracks was a safety feature and also allowed east-west bound automobiles and streetcars to move without being stopped by the constant arrivals and departures of trains. (Jefferson County. Postcard in the collections of the ADAH.)

Steam locomotives have passed into the legend of America. Pictured here circa 1935 is a crew in the Southern Railway Yard at Anniston. (Calhoun County. Courtesy of the Russell Collection, Public Library of Anniston and Calhoun County.)

"The Lightning Route," as Montgomerians called the trolley system of the Capital City Street Railway Company, was the first electric trolley system in the United States. Joseph Arthur Gaboury, a Canadian engineer, and Charles Van Depoele, a Belgian electrical engineer, first tested their invention shortly after midnight on March 25, 1886. The *Montgomery Advertiser* reported that "four trips were made up and down Commerce Street and the car moved as easily and smoothly as a ghost in the clear moonlight." On April 15, regular passenger service was initiated. (Montgomery County. ADAH.)

In March 1885, Choccolocco Street in Oxford was crowded with various forms of transportation. (Calhoun County. ADAH.)

Joe Brunner of Cullman proudly stands by his new 1940 Ford. So important had the automobile become that family albums across the state include snapshots of family members posed with their cars, just as late nineteenth and early twentieth century families posed with their wagons and other important possessions. (Cullman County. Courtesy of Rickie Louise Brunner.)

In 1910, the Birmingham *Ledger* sponsored a "Good roads tour of Alabama." Here a group paused at the top of Birmingham's Red Mountain on the way to Montgomery. The trip took an entire day. By the end of the 1920s, automobiles had opened up Alabama's rural areas and changed the urban landscape of its towns. (Jefferson County. Courtesy of Special Collection, Samford University Library.)

After the boll weevil devastated Alabama cotton, farmers were forced to diversify. Truck farming became an important way for farmers to increase their profits. (ADAH.)

Coca Cola, primarily associated with Atlanta, actually was invented in Columbus, Georgia. Trucks, like those parked at the Mobile Coca-Cola Bottling Company at 200 North Royal Street, were used to deliver the bottles of the popular drink to drug and grocery stores, as well as to filling stations. (Mobile County. Courtesy of the University of South Alabama Archives.)

Modern highways opened isolated rural areas of the state and facilitated the movement of goods and people around Alabama. They also reflected an increasingly transient society where people no longer grew up and lived their lives in the same community as their parents, grandparents, and great-grandparents. This U.S. highway in Morgan County, beautified as part of a 1930s CWA project, runs through the flat rich farmland of the Tennessee Valley. (Morgan County. ADAH.)

came to the state. Economic exploitation of the state's large deposits of ore and minerals was made possible by capital investment by both native and outside industrialists and by railroads, especially the Louisville and Nashville network. Railroads were built where navigable rivers did not flow, and they soon replaced steamboats. The state's industrial growth was supported by the extensive development of railroads, especially in and around the mineral district near Birmingham.

In the late twentieth century railroads were partly supplanted by automobiles and trucks traveling interstate highways. Rivers, extended by locks and dredging, became important again for industry and commerce, the manufacture of hydroelectric power, and recreational activities. No understanding of Alabama would be complete without taking into account the state's rivers, the boats that moved on them, the bridges that spanned them, the power they generated, and the many activities associated with them.

Alabama was also on the cutting edge of aviation and aerospace development. The Wright brothers, Orville and Wilbur, operated a flight school in Montgomery, and many pilots who flew in the infant U.S. air corps during World War I trained in Alabama. The state's mild climate and large areas of flat land in the south were perfect for flight training. Again in World War II, hundreds of pilots trained at Maxwell, Gunter, and Craig Fields. Following the war touch-and-go training air fields dotted the rural countryside, and many were turned into small-town airports, while commercial aviation increased in major cities.

Although the Civil Works Administration (CWA) was created to put Americans to work during the Depression, the work the CWA tackled was anything but "made" work. This work crew built a new bridge to replace an old one over the Sipsey River in Winston County in the mid-1930s. (Winston County. ADAH.)

Tourist camps began dotting the Alabama landscape in the 1930s and 1940s in direct response to improved highways and more automobiles. The Ideal Court, located at 2095 Hall's Mill Road in Mobile, was photographed on March 24, 1941. (Mobile County. Courtesy of the University of South Alabama Archives.)

Wilbur and Orville Wright operated a flight school in Montgomery at the Kohn Plantation, which later became part of Maxwell Field. In late March 1910, the pioneering aviators tested their latest airplane. (Montgomery County. ADAH.)

Responding to the burgeoning interest in aviation, Civil Works Administration workers improved airfields across the state. Despite the popularity of flying, early airfields were little more than graded dirt fields. This was a "view down the long runway" at the Geneva Airport in the mid-1930s. (Geneva County. ADAH.)

This aerial view of the Birmingham Municipal Airport was made during the National Air Carnival in June 1941. After the Japanese attacked Pearl Harbor later that year, the Bechtel–McCone Aircraft Modification Company opened a factory at the airport where one-half of all the B-29 bombers used during the war were equipped and modified. (Jefferson County. ADAH.)

On June 1, 1945, Eastern Air Lines inaugurated its Chicago to Miami and Memphis to Miami service which included a stop at Montgomery's Dannelly Field. (Montgomery County. ADAH.)

At the end of the nineteenth century, the ruins of the old Tannehill blast furnace that was destroyed in the Civil War had become a popular place for weekend outings. Today a historical park on the site commemorates the history of the iron industry in the state. (Bibb and Tuscaloosa Counties. Courtesy of Special Collection, Samford University Library.)

# six
*Industry*

In the antebellum period, Alabama industry developed along the lines of other Southern states with modest beginnings in textiles and iron production utilizing slave as well as white laborers. Daniel Pratt, a transplanted native of New Hampshire, was Alabama's most successful pre–Civil War industrialist. In the 1830s, Pratt established a factory north of Montgomery to manufacture cotton gins. The factory developed into the self-sufficient industrial village of Prattville. Although Pratt diversified his investments, producing textiles, as well as carriages, windows, doors, and blinds, his fortune was based on the manufacture and sale of cotton gins. Because of his efforts, in 1859 Alabama led the nation in manufacturing gins. Pratt preached the virtue of industrialization, but Alabama was a cotton state, and while cotton prices remained high his pleas went largely unheeded.

In 1856, the Alabama Coal Mining Company near Montevallo became the state's first modern underground mining operation, and Joseph Squire, its English-born manager, pioneered the opening of Alabama coal fields. The Civil War accelerated Alabama's industrial development, and its effect stimulated coal mining and prompted an expansion of Alabama's primitive iron industry. By 1865, the

Coal mining was dirty and dangerous work, but coal production was critical to the industrial development of Alabama. Coal miners in the 1930s endured low pay and public hostility to unions and strikes. Black lung and other respiratory diseases plagued the men who spent their days underground. This photograph of Chester "Chuck" Latham, a mine foreman at Carbon Hill, gave a human face to an important industry. (Walker County. Courtesy of the Library of Congress.)

The ironworks at Ironton (present-day Irondale) in Shades Valley circa 1880 included a superintendent's house, a hotel, and cabins for laborers behind beehive coke ovens. This ironworks, which supplied iron to Selma for Confederate cannons, was destroyed by Northern raiders during the Civil War and rebuilt soon after the war ended. (Jefferson County. ADAH.)

The production of pig iron was the foundation of Birmingham's industrial development. The Sloss City Furnaces were among the many plants which used Jefferson County coal, iron ore, and limestone to produce iron. By World War I, Sloss-Sheffield Steel and Iron Company, as it was by then known, was the largest producer of pig iron in the world. By 1971, the oldest remaining blast furnaces in the city were shut down due to obsolescence and a declining market. The furnaces now are a National Historic Landmark and a museum of the City of Birmingham. (Jefferson County. ADAH.)

Company towns had company stores, operated for the convenience of the workers and to make profits for the companies. Workers often were paid in scrip which could be redeemed only at the company store. The Tennessee Coal, Iron and Railroad Company's Ensley Store circa 1930 was typical. (Jefferson County. Courtesy of the Library of Congress.)

The Tennessee Coal, Iron and Railroad Company led Alabama steel production and continued to dominate after it was absorbed by the United States Steel Corporation in 1907. (Jefferson County. Courtesy of the Birmingham Public Library Department of Archives and Manuscripts.)

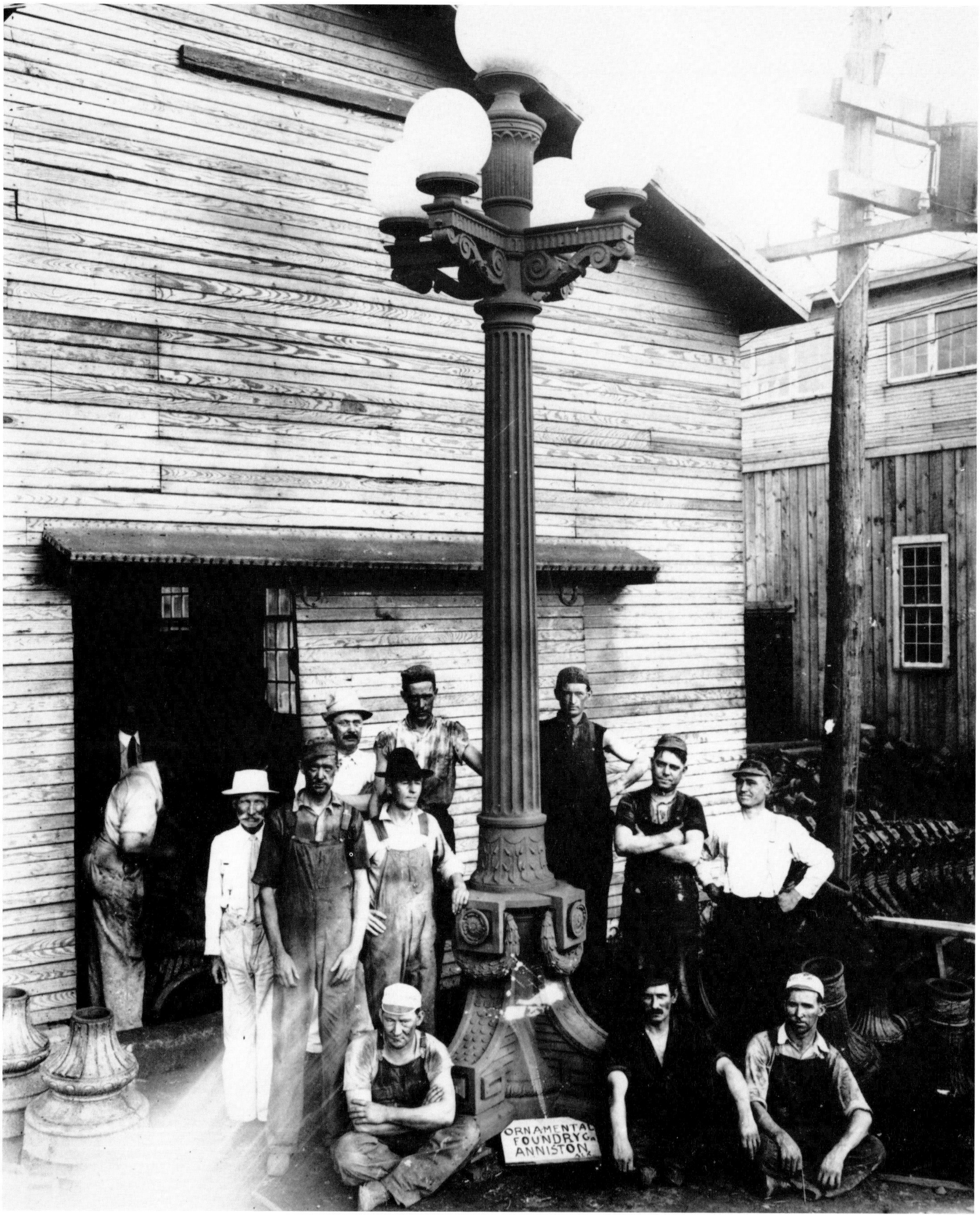
ORNAMENTAL
FOUNDRY Co.
ANNISTON

Throughout the 1920s, mass employment for women remained confined to textiles and the clothing industry. Women seamstresses in Mobile paused for the photographer. (Mobile County. Courtesy of the University of South Alabama Archives.)

Left: This streetlight was a finished product made from Birmingham iron ore at the Ornamental Foundry Company in Anniston. The Foundry's advertising in 1913–14 boasted that this ornamental streetlighting was "that mark of modern progressiveness [that] should be investigated by every municipality." It already could be seen in Washington, D.C.; Brooklyn; and Providence, Rhode Island; as well as in Birmingham, Troy, Dothan, Tuscaloosa, and Decatur in Alabama. World War I soon diverted iron and steel to military needs. (Calhoun County. Courtesy of the Russell Collection, Public Library of Anniston and Calhoun County.)

In the early years of the twentieth century, Continental Gin Company in Prattville was, as the postcard boosts, the largest gin works in the world. (Autauga County. Postcard from the collections of the ADAH.)

Members of the Kiwanis Club of Alexander City visited the Avondale Mills circa 1924 at the invitation of J. F. Comer, oldest son of Governor B. B. Comer. (Tallapoosa County. Courtesy of Judge C. J. Coley.)

area east and south of present-day Birmingham had sixteen blast furnaces using iron ore, limestone, and charcoal as their basic materials.

Federal raids destroyed the infant coal and iron industry, but it was revived in the 1870s. In 1871, Colonel James R. Powell's Elyton Land Company laid out the city blocks and lots of Birmingham. After a relatively slow beginning, an industrial boom came in the 1880s. Revolutionary new manufacturing techniques, as well as such colorful investors and competitors as Henry DeBardeleben (Daniel Pratt's son-in-law), Enoch Ensley, Truman Aldrich, James Bowron, Erskine Ramsay, and James Sloss, fueled the growth that gave Birmingham the sobriquet the "Magic City."

By 1876, coke pig iron of good quality was being made, and, by 1889, Alabama was the nation's fourth largest producer of iron. By 1900, the state produced more than 1 million tons of iron a year and exported three-fourths of all pig iron shipped from the United States. There were numerous corporate mergers among the businesses of the mineral district, but the Tennessee Coal, Iron and Railroad Company, known as TCI, emerged as the giant. However, when the United States Steel Corporation absorbed TCI in 1907, any dreams that Southern corporations might threaten Pittsburgh's dominant position were ended.

The Alabama coal industry employed native whites and blacks, with blacks always in the majority, and in 1890 foreign-born workers made up 18.7 percent of the work force. Despite low wages, poor working conditions, and competition from convict labor, Alabamians flocked to the mines. They preferred company benefits and regular pay, even if it was in company scrip, to the privations of tenant farming.

Convict labor had been adopted by Alabama to reduce the cost of prisons and to supplement the

New Deal legislation protected the rights of workers to organize unions. Labor Day picnics and parades were important social events where politicians often appeared to campaign. Auxiliary 694 of the Textile Workers Union of America prepared for a Labor Day parade in 1948. (Montgomery County. ADAH.)

From the 1840s to the present, the textile industry has flourished in Alabama. Although the workers in this Huntsville mill were men, textile mills across the state employed large numbers of women. (Madison County. Courtesy of the Huntsville–Madison County Public Library.)

Quarries at Sylacauga yield beautiful Alabama marble used in buildings in Alabama and across the United States. Dr. Edward Gantt, a physician who traveled through the Mississippi Territory with General Andrew Jackson in 1814, is generally credited with discovering the marble deposit in what is now Talladega County. He had located an outcropping of the purest white marble in the world. In the 1830s, several quarries opened in the area. By 1906, several New Yorkers had purchased the quarry originally owned by Gantt and developed it into a marble-working center later called the Alabama Marble Company. Sylacauga marble has been used in the Lincoln Memorial, the Washington Monument, the U.S. Supreme Court Building, the Alabama Department of Archives and History building in Montgomery, the House chamber in the U.S. Capitol, and the famous duck fountain in the lobby of the Peabody Hotel in Memphis. (Talladega County. Courtesy of the B. B. Comer Memorial Library.)

In the forests above Mobile, logging became an important industry. Teams of oxen hauled logs to tram railroads which then carried the logs to Mobile. This logging railroad in the piney woods, circa 1895, brought the trains to the trees. (Courtesy of the University of South Alabama Archives)

Pulpwood and paper production are important in a state with so much land in forests. This pulpwood on the Styx River was ready to be sent to the paper mill when in was photographed by Dorothea Lange as part of her work on the Alabama Writers' Project in the 1930s. (Baldwin County. Courtesy of the Library of Congress.)

Thomas W. Martin became president of the Alabama Power Company in 1920. Under his leadership, the utility company expanded its planned series of six hydroelectric dams, as well as its influence in the state legislature. Martin was photographed at Lock 18 at Jordan Dam in 1927. (Elmore County. Courtesy of Alabama Power Company Corporate Archives.)

A crowd gathered for the dedication of Lock 12 at Lay Dam on November 23, 1929. (Chilton and Coosa Counties. Courtesy of Alabama Power Company Corporate Archives.)

work force. Prisoners were put up for "rent" to mining and timber companies on a bid basis, but the cruelties of the convict-lease system were a scandal. Despite protests from reform groups, profits derived by the corporations, by the state, and by those counties that participated overrode questions of humanitarianism and justice, and leasing was not abandoned until 1928.

If the growth of industry produced enormous wealth for a few and middle-class professional opportunities for others, it also engendered a union movement. Organized labor was stronger in Alabama than in any other Southern state. The Knights of Labor appeared in Alabama in the late 1870s, prospered briefly in the 1880s, but ultimately failed because of internal division and external resistance.

In 1890, Alabama coal miners affiliated with the United Mine Workers and launched a turbulent era marked by sporadic strikes that usually failed. In the 1890s, 1910s, 1919, and 1920–1921, the miners struck. They lost each time because of management's superior resources, which included importing strikebreakers and using convict labor. The strikers were further disadvantaged by public hostility and opposition from unsympathetic state authorities who utilized national guard units to break strikes.

The union movement underwent sporadic reorganization, but declined greatly by the 1920s, only to be revived again under New Deal pro-labor legislation. Organized labor became an important liberal force in state politics from the 1930s into the 1960s but lost some of its strength in Alabama in the last decades of the twentieth century.

Besides its large role in coal, iron, and steel production, Alabama developed an important textile industry. In the antebellum period, advocates of industry and diversification argued that it made

The port of Mobile opened Alabama to the world. In this circa 1936 photograph, ships were being unloaded at the state docks. (Mobile County. Courtesy of the University of South Alabama Archives.)

Below: Wilson Dam at Muscle Shoals became the first link in the Tennessee Valley Authority's chain of dams. President Franklin D. Roosevelt incorporated the dam into the TVA system in 1933. The TVA revolutionized the life of residents in the area by bringing cheap electricity to their homes and farms. (Colbert County. ADAH.)

economic sense to manufacture cotton cloth where the fiber was grown. By 1860 the state had sixteen small mills whose labor force of 1,312 workers was 59 percent female. The textile industry suffered during the Civil War and Reconstruction, but there was a strong resurgence in the 1880s. By 1900, Alabama had thirty-one mills capitalized at $11,638,757 with 8,332 workers almost equally divided between men and women. Children under sixteen made up 29 percent of the laborers.

The textile industry was scattered in small units across the state and employed mostly white workers. Early working conditions often were poor, and pay

The Mobile dry docks and shipbuilding companies grew so rapidly during World War II that the city suffered a critical shortage of housing for workers. (Mobile County. Courtesy of the University of South Alabama Archives.)

World War II created many new job opportunities for women. With so many young men at war, businesses and industries hired women workers for traditionally male jobs. At Redstone Arsenal, women worked on an assembly line packing shells. (Madison County. Courtesy of U.S. Army Missile Command, Redstone Arsenal.)

was low. In the 1930s, unionized textile workers in Alabama took part in a national strike, but they faced the same obstacles that confronted the coal miners, and they also lost. Despite conflict, the textile industry grew, adding diversification to the state's economy and providing employment for many citizens. In 1950, 54,000 workers were employed in seventy-two textile mills, the largest of which was the Avondale Mills Corporation founded by the Comer family. Other mills are significant, especially Benjamin Russell's mills headquartered at Alexander City. Specializing in athletic wear, Russell's products are sold internationally and illustrate the continued importance of textiles as a major industry in Alabama.

Other industries also grew in the twentieth century. New equipment and sophisticated techniques by the Alabama Dry Dock and Shipbuilding Company at Mobile and the vital space program at Huntsville revolutionized the local economies and brought the state international attention. Huntsville has played a significant role in the nation's defense program and became a center of high technological growth in Alabama. Spin-off industries from aerospace and defense have become a major component of Alabama's economy. New endeavors and industries—tires, construction, and automobiles as exemplified by the giant commitment of Mercedes-Benz to the Tuscaloosa area—are legitimate reasons for optimism about Alabama's future.

The dynamics of Alabama industrial and manufacturing history—including the backgrounds of its blue-collar workers, labor unions, and foreign-born laborers—have made it ethnically and economically different from other Deep South states, and this cultural diversity has enriched the heritage of the state.

The decision by German automobile manufacturer Mercedes-Benz to locate in Tuscaloosa County near Vance was cheered by Alabamians as a significant recognition by others of the state's assets and potential. This billboard welcomed Mercedes-Benz officials to the site of their future plant in 1993. (Tuscaloosa County. ADAH.)

Below: Huntsville Arsenal and Redstone Arsenal produced artillery shells and bombs during World War II. Then, in 1950, the U.S. Army began to concentrate rocket development at Redstone Arsenal. In 1956, the Army Ballistic Agency was established at Redstone, marking dramatic changes that were realized by the 1960s. The National Aeronautics and Space Administration (NASA) created the George C. Marshall Space Flight Center under Wernher von Braun in 1958, and a combination of American and German scientists developed rocket engines there. At the local level, Huntsville benefited from the economy's upsurge, as advanced military and space research helped spawn a number of new, high-technology industries. (Madison County. ADAH.)

Fireworks lit the sky—and stars again fell on Alabama—during the celebration for opening the newly renovated Capitol in Montgomery in December 1992. (Courtesy of Rus Baxley Photography, P.O. Box 6092, Montgomery, Al 36106.)

During the tenth century A.D., the Mississippian culture, which had evolved in the central Mississippi River valley, spread to central Alabama. This was the highest cultural achievement in the prehistoric Southeast. Pottery making flourished during this period with the introduction of shell tempering. Some types of Mississippian artifacts, including gorgets made from shell, reflected beliefs about ancestors, deities, warfare, and the afterlife. By the Protohistoric Period (1550–1680), pottery from the upper Alabama River region, like this painted bowl, had become quite distinctive. During the Historic Period, effigy figures and other items sometimes were made from copper traded to the Indians by European settlers. Glass beads also were popular trade items during the Historic Period. (Artifacts from the collections of the ADAH.)

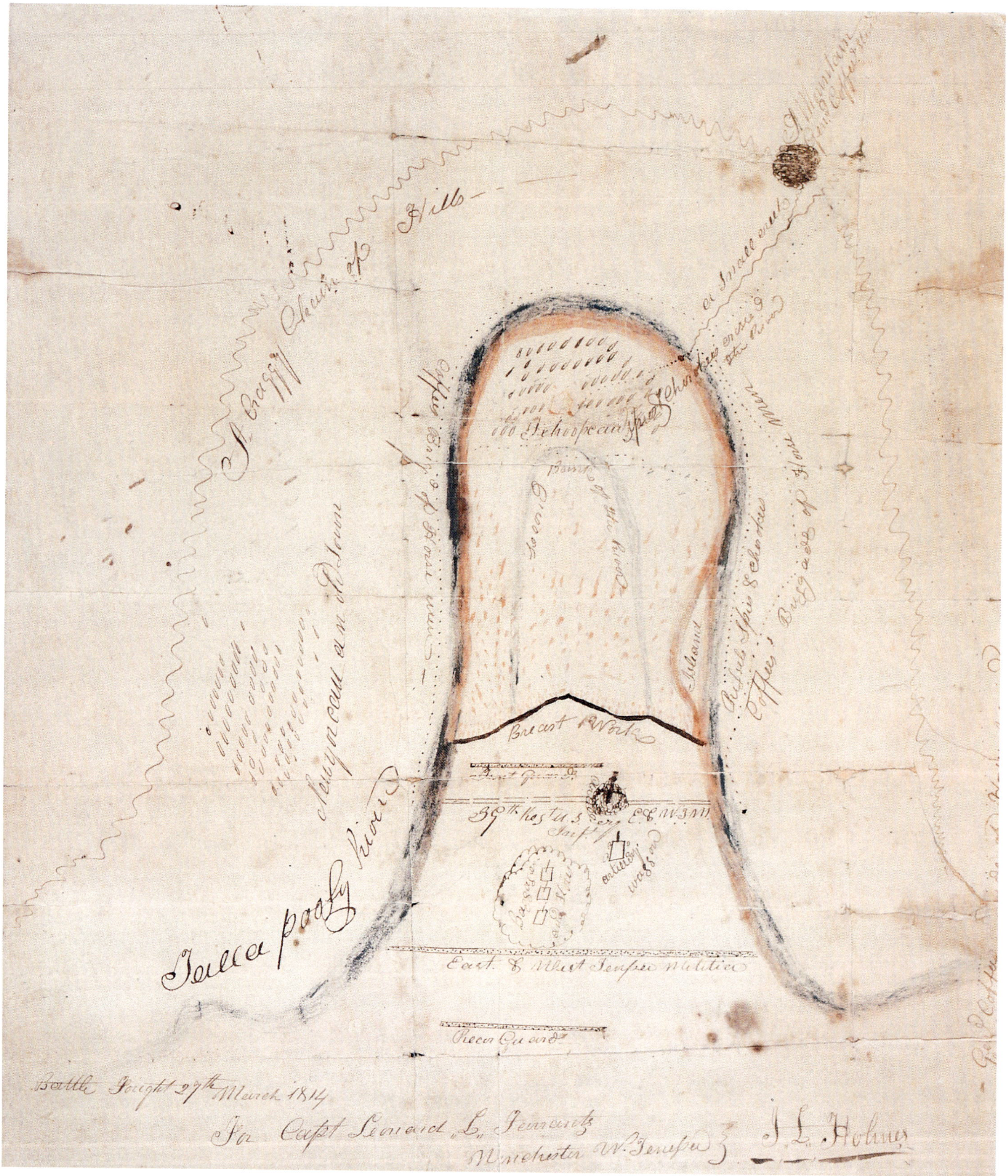
Breast Work
Rear Guard
East & West Tennessee Militia
Tallapoosy River
Hills
Battle Fought 27th March 1814
J. L. Holmes

Alabama's first constitution was written in Huntsville in 1819. Today, a reconstructed village and a living history museum illustrate life in early Alabama. (Madison County. Courtesy of Alabama Constitution Village.)

Right: The victory of Andrew Jackson's militia at the Battle of Horseshoe Bend on March 27, 1814, destroyed the power of the Creeks and opened more Indian lands for settlement. Over eight hundred Indians were killed in the battle. Fewer than fifty of Jackson's militiamen and their Indian allies died in the fight. Sam Houston, a young Tennessee Volunteer, wrote that when the sun went down that day, "it set over the ruin of the Creek Nation." The defeat at Horseshoe Bend ultimately led to the cession of the remaining Creek lands and the forced resettlement by 1840 of most Creeks to lands west of the Mississippi River. (Tallapoosa County. Map from the collections of the ADAH.)

William McIntosh, a Lower Creek Indian headman who was part Scottish, supported the United States government and played a leading role in the land cessions of 1814, 1818, 1821, and 1825. By signing the 1825 Treaty of Indian Springs, McIntosh broke a Creek law forbidding further land cessions to the Americans. Before dawn on the day after he signed the treaty, Upper Creek Indians executed him. This portrait was painted by Nathan Negus, an itinerant painter originally from Petersham, Massachusetts, who, with his brother Joseph, established a successful business in Eatonton, Georgia. Sometime in 1821 or 1822, Negus traveled to Indian Springs, home of the Creek nation, to paint this larger-than-life size portrait of McIntosh which measures 90 by 55 inches. (Portrait from the collections of the ADAH.)

Work began on Kirkwood Mansion in Eutaw in the late 1850s. David R. Anthony was the possible contractor who built the house for Foster M. Kirksey, a local planter and merchant. With the advent of the Civil War, work on the mansion was interrupted. The cast-iron railing for the balcony was not installed, and the interior finish was simplified. When the house was restored in 1973–1979, the balcony railing and decorative interior plaster cornices were added to finish work begun over one hundred years earlier. (Greene County. Photograph by Dan Brothers. Courtesy of the Alabama Bureau of Tourism and Travel.)

The Kymulga Grist Mill was built in 1864 by slave labor. It was restored in 1988, and corn is still ground as part of the mill operation. The mill is located next to the Kymulga Covered Bridge over Talladega Creek. (Talladega County. Photograph by Dan Brothers. Courtesy of the Alabama Bureau of Tourism and Travel.)

The flag commonly recognized today as the Confederate battle flag is actually a variant of the flag which was originally issued for use by the Army of Northern Virginia. By the end of the war, modified versions of this flag were being used throughout the Confederacy. However, the flag with the St. Andrew's cross was just one of many different battle flags used by the military. The three pictured here were all in use at the same time and were all recognized by the men who carried them as "the" battle flag.

The flag of the Eighteenth Alabama Infantry was captured by Union forces at the Battle of Missionary Ridge on November 25, 1863. It was returned by the U.S. War Department in 1905. (Flag from the collections of the ADAH.)

The flag of the Thirteenth Alabama Infantry, third wool bunting Army of Northern Virginia issue, was captured on July 3, 1863, at the Battle of Gettysburg. The U.S. War Department returned the flag to the state of Alabama in 1905. (Flag from the collections of the ADAH.)

Federal troops captured the flag of the Twenty-second Alabama Infantry at the Battle of Chickamauga on September 20, 1863. The flag was returned to Alabama by the state of Ohio in 1972. (Flag from the collections of the ADAH.)

This portrait of an unidentified African-American woman is from the Mary Lee Simpson photograph collection. Around 1900, Simpson photographed the people of Furman, a rural Wilcox County community. Simpson's work includes character studies and photographic records of such daily domestic activities as washing clothes and sweeping the yard. The photographs, all beautifully hand-tinted, are equally valuable as works of art and historical documentation. (Wilcox County. ADAH.)

Helen Keller was born at Ivy Green in Tuscumbia in 1880. A childhood illness left the two-year-old Helen blind and deaf; however, through her courage and the perseverance of her teacher, Annie Sullivan, she triumphed over her disabilities. She became a noted author, speaker, and advocate for individuals with disabilities. Helen Keller died in 1968. Ivy Green, the Keller family home built in the 1820s, is now a museum of the city of Tuscumbia. (Colbert County. Photograph by Dan Brothers. Courtesy of the Alabama Bureau of Tourism and Travel.)

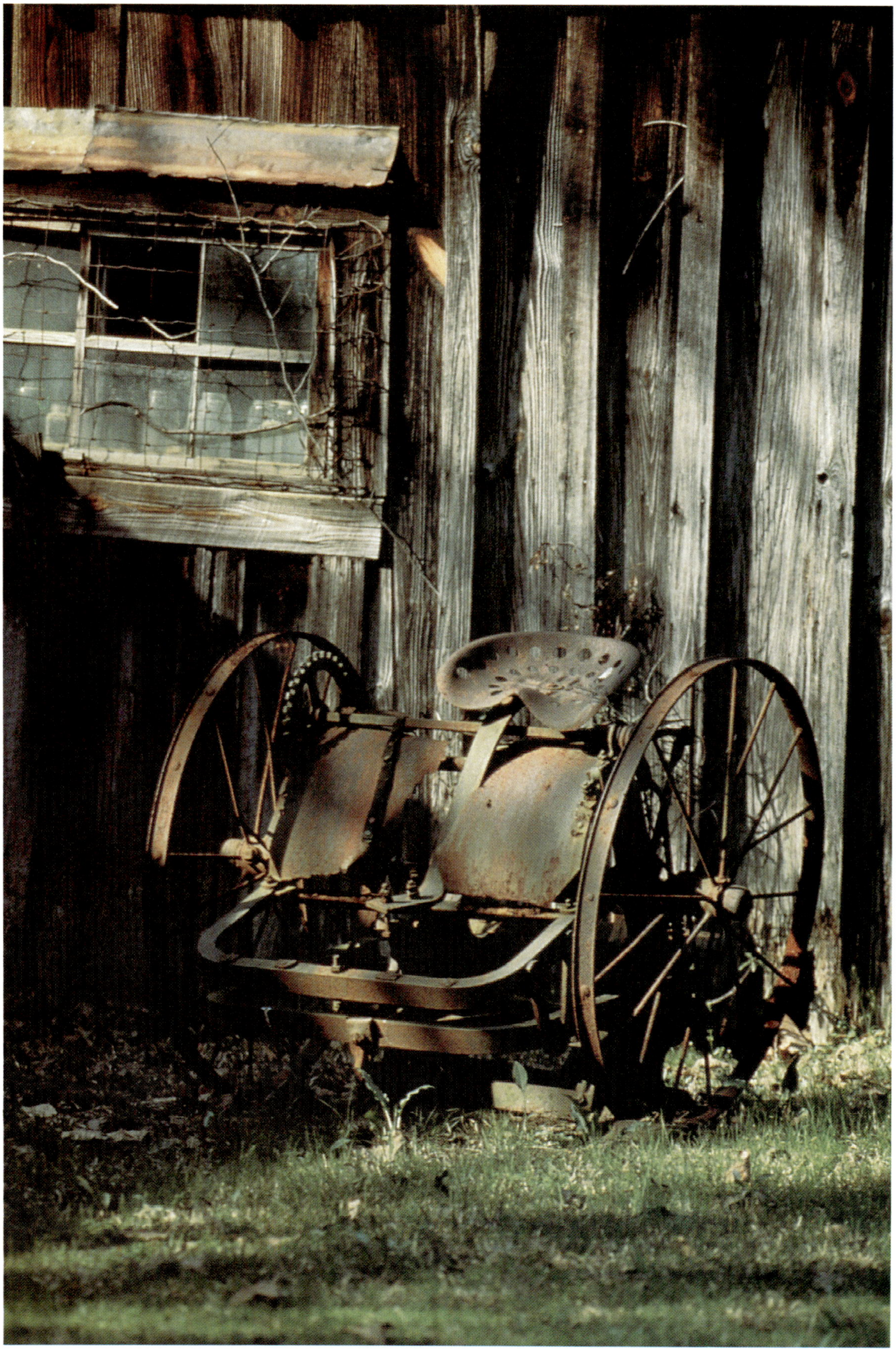

Bellingrath Gardens and Home encompasses 900 acres on the Isle aux Oies River. The house was once home to industrialist Walter D. Bellingrath who bought the land in 1918 as a fishing camp. Today, the house is surrounded by a 65-acre garden and filled with an extensive collection of antique furniture, porcelains, and china. (Mobile County. Photograph by Dan Brothers. Courtesy of the Alabama Bureau of Tourism and Travel.)

Left: Old farm machinery, like this 1950s stalk cutter, lying idle at rural homes and farms across the state provides testimony and a tangible link to Alabama's agricultural roots. (Photograph by Mark Morrison. Courtesy of Alabama Farmers Federation.)

The USS *Alabama* Battleship Memorial Park is one of Alabama's top tourist attractions. The centerpiece of the park is the battleship that won nine battle stars during World War II. (Mobile County. Photograph by Dan Brothers. Courtesy of the Alabama Bureau of Tourism and Travel.)

The Talladega Superspeedway hosts two major NASCAR Winston Cup events each year: the Winston 500 in May and the DieHard 500, pictured in July 1994. (Talladega County. Photograph by Dan Brothers. Courtesy of the Alabama Bureau of Tourism and Travel.)

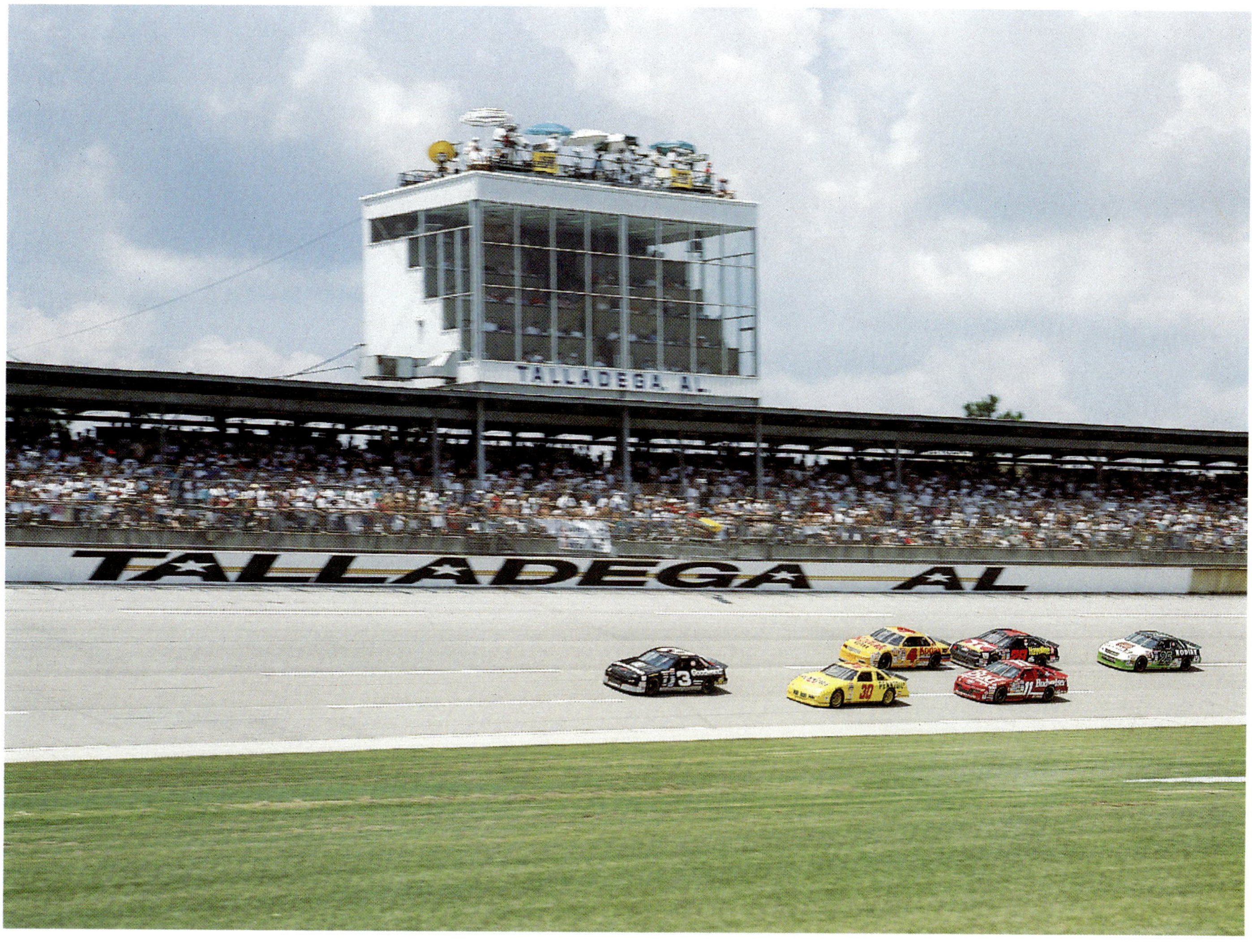
TALLADEGA, AL.
TALLADEGA AL

In 1989, the University of Alabama football team played its first game ever on the Auburn University campus. The crowd in the stadium so swelled the population of the town that, for that one day, Auburn was the fifth largest city in the state. The mixture of red and white and orange and blue shakers reflected the divided nature of the rivalry within families and even dating couples. (Lee County. Courtesy of the Auburn University Photographic Services.)

The city of Florence hosts the annual W. C. Handy Music Festival in honor of the musical legacy of Handy, "Father of the Blues." William Christopher Handy, born in 1873, wrote "St. Louis Blues," "Memphis Blues," "Beale Street Blues," and dozens of other songs that captivated audiences in the early decades of the twentieth century. The log cabin in which Handy was born is now part of the W. C. Handy Birthplace, Museum and Library, a Florence city museum. (Lauderdale County. Photograph by Dan Brothers. Courtesy of the Alabama Bureau of Tourism and Travel.)

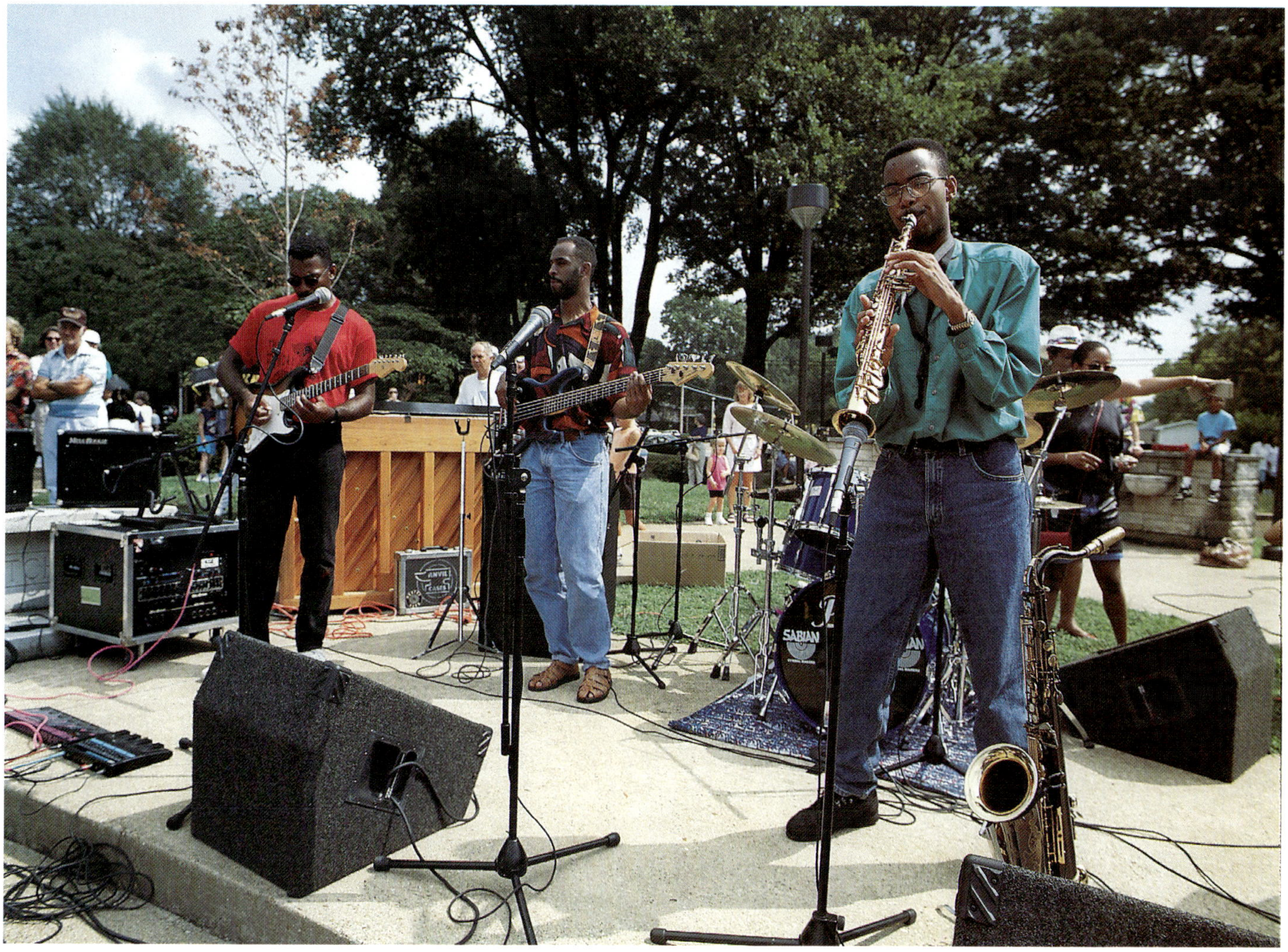
SABIAN

The Alabama Shakespeare Festival in Montgomery offers world-class classical and contemporary theatrical productions and educational programs on a year-round basis. The complex, located in the Wynton Blount Cultural Park, attracts over 250,000 visitors annually. (Montgomery County. Photograph by Dan Brothers. Courtesy of the Alabama Bureau of Tourism and Travel.)

# seven
*The Growth of Cities*

Mobile, with a population of almost 30,000 in 1860, was the largest city of antebellum Alabama. Montgomery stood second with 8,843 people, and then Tuscaloosa (3,989), Huntsville (3,634), and Selma (3,177). The rural nature of Alabama's population continued after the Civil War.

Urbanization came with the development of industry and improvements in transportation and with the expansion of older cities and the rise in importance of industrial cities in the north such as Birmingham, Anniston, and Gadsden. Even small towns changed as Alabamians became less dependent on agriculture for their livelihood and more reliant on a diversity of occupations, including light and heavy industry, countless service jobs, and the professions. Although a community connected to an industry, like Daniel Pratt's town, had antebellum origins, industrial growth spawned many new company towns and mill villages, especially around coal mines and steel and textile mills.

Population growth in cities and towns across the state has been phenomenal. Jefferson County grew from 12,235 people in 1870 to 88,501 in 1890. By 1920 Birmingham was the third largest city in the South behind New Orleans and Atlanta. Local boosters

By the early twentieth century, the major cities in Alabama were thriving commercial and business centers. Dauphin Street in Mobile in the late 1920s was the location of a variety of businesses offering services or entertainment to Mobilians and residents from nearby communities. (Mobile County. ADAH.)

touted Tallassee as the "future Lowell of the South," and New South promoters saw nothing but unlimited horizons for Cullman, Sheffield, Bessemer, Fort Payne, and Decatur, which some said was destined to be the "Chicago of the South."

The growth of cities brought its own special problems such as supplying citizens a variety of services—clean water, sewage disposal, police, fire and health protection, transportation, electricity, and education. But with urbanization came new opportunities—economic and cultural—for Alabama citizens.

In 1882, the Huntsville City Hall also housed commercial establishments such as A. Adler's Dry Goods and Groceries. (Madison County. ADAH.)

The town of Huntsville grew up around the big spring where John Hunt built his cabin about 1805. Stories of early settlers tell of the large number of giant rattlesnakes that inhabited the rocks around the spring and how many years it took to rid the spring area of snakes. (Madison County. Courtesy of the Birmingham Public Library Department of Archives and Manuscripts.)

The turn of the century was cause for celebrations across the state. In Montgomery, several businesses participated in the festivities that went on for months. The "Famous Fin de Siècle Comb" must have been quite an attraction since it was so prominently advertised outside Goetter's department store. (Montgomery County. ADAH.)

This is the often photographed view looking from the fountain at Court Square up Dexter Avenue to the state Capitol. This picture was taken circa 1940. (Montgomery County. ADAH.)

Right: Birmingham had become a city following the great iron boom of the 1880s. This was Nineteenth Street looking north from First Avenue. (Jefferson County. Courtesy of the Birmingham Public Library Department of Archives and Manuscripts.)

The local millinery shop was an important business for the women of any town. This one in Aliceville, circa 1890, combined millinery with a florist shop. (Pickens County. Courtesy of the Aliceville Public Library.)

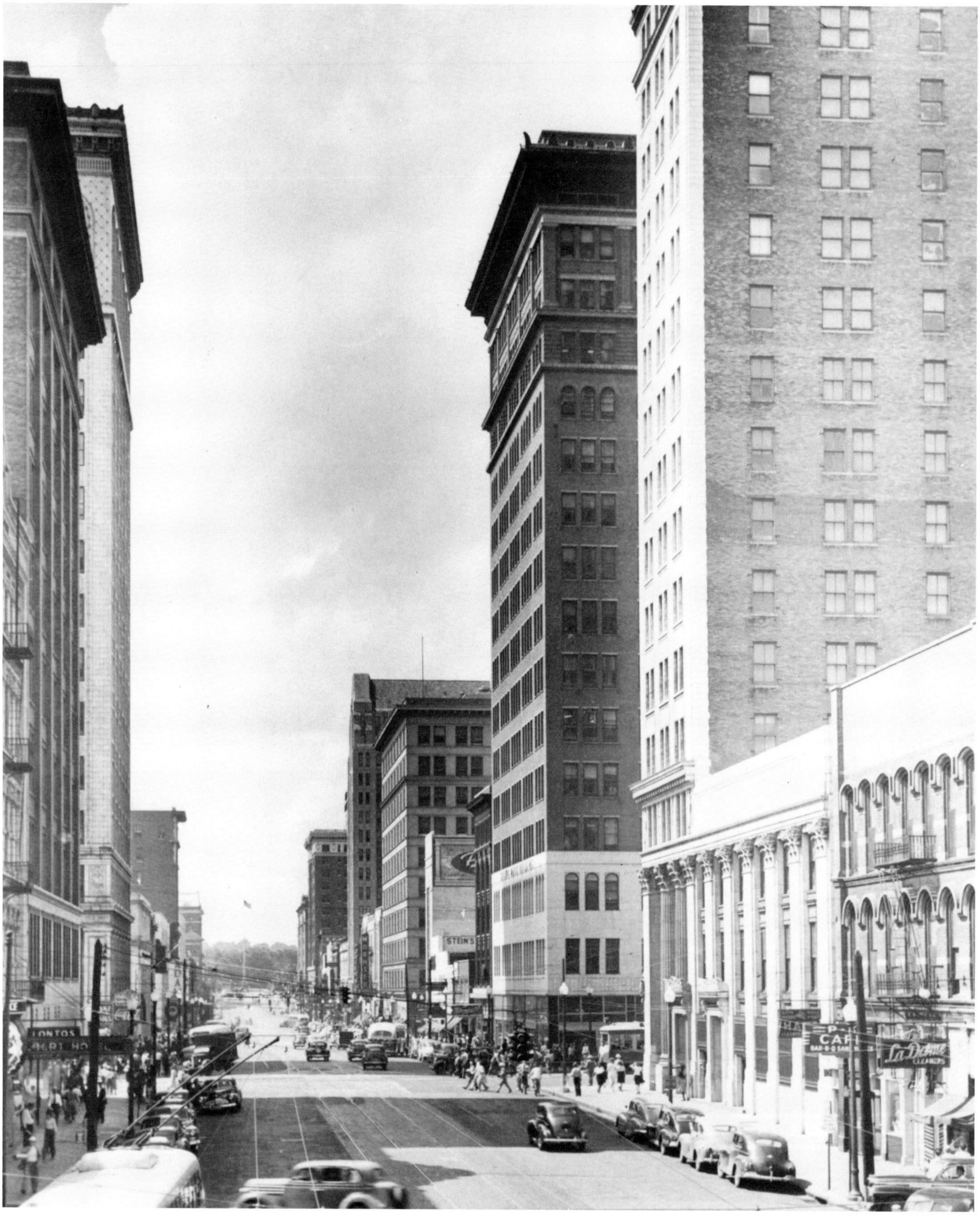
STEIN'S

The small neighborhood grocery store was the last link in the chain of food distribution for the first half of the twentieth century. Many of these stores allowed customers to call in their orders and have their groceries delivered by boys on bicycles. This is Charles Boldone's Meats and Groceries in Birmingham. (Jefferson County. Courtesy of the Birmingham Public Library Department of Archives and Manuscripts.)

Gunn's Pharmacy, at the corner of Third Avenue North and Eighteenth Street in Birmingham, sold tickets to the Alabama State Fair. The large electric sign encouraged shoppers circa 1915 to "drink at our fountain." On the floors above the pharmacy, Covell's Photo Studio offered portraits, copies, and enlargements. (Jefferson County. ADAH.)

Left: When the streets of Birmingham were drawn in Benjamin P. Worthington's cornfield in 1871, Colonel James R. Powell, president of the Elyton Land Company which founded the city, had the surveyor create a block square park on the rise overlooking Twentieth Street. He named it Capitol Park because he believed it was only a matter of time before the capital of Alabama would be moved from Montgomery to the "Magic City" in Jefferson County. The park was renamed Wilson Park after World War I. This photograph shows the intersection of First Avenue and Twentieth Street in the foreground with the American flag flying in the park at the end of the street. By 1913, four skyscrapers had been built at this intersection of Birmingham's main thoroughfares, winning for it the distinction of "the heaviest corner on earth." (Jefferson County. Courtesy of the Birmingham Public Library Archives.)

Gault Street in the northeast Alabama town of Fort Payne vividly illustrated the transition to modern times in the early decades of the twentieth century. Mules and wagons and horses and buggies vied with automobiles for space on the streets. (DeKalb County. Courtesy of Collins Kirby and Landmarks of DeKalb County, Inc.)

This view of Broad Street in Camden was typical of Black Belt county seats and many smaller towns across Alabama around the turn of the century. (Wilcox County. Courtesy of the Wilcox County Library.)

Toomer's Corner (to the right of the tree) was named for Sheldon Toomer who operated a drug store there in the 1890s. It was a meeting place for the town of Auburn and the campus of the Alabama Agricultural and Mechanical College which became the Alabama Polytechnic Institute in 1899. Today, the corner is known for pep rallies, political speeches, and victory celebrations. (Lee County. Courtesy of the Auburn University Archives.)

Highway intersections, such as this one on the Glenwood to Luverne Road in Crenshaw County, grew into local centers of commercial activity. This photograph was taken in the mid-1930s. (Crenshaw County. ADAH.)

Early filling stations provided full automotive services to its customers. The Windham Service Station and a Chevrolet dealership, owned by Cary Walker, were located on the corner of Columbus and Pickens Streets in Kennedy. This picture was taken circa 1927. (Lamar County. Courtesy of Margene Walker.)

Right: Sarver's Store in Athens, circa 1910, provided customers with a wide range of products. (Limestone County. Courtesy of the Auburn University Center for the Arts and Humanities.)

Emil Kroessman, a professional photographer who lived in Tell City, Indiana, photographed several Alabama businesses in 1910. His pictures covered a wide variety of retail operations, including grocers, department stores, and general merchandise stores in Wetumpka, Brewton, Prattville, and Greenville. Barbershops, such as this one Kroessman photographed in Prattville, offered men shaves, hair cuts, and conversation. (Autauga County. ADAH.)

The interior of Toomer's Drug Store was typical of an early twentieth century establishment. The soda fountain became famous for its special fresh-squeezed lemonade. (Lee County. Courtesy of the Auburn University Center for the Arts and Humanities.)

The American Laundry Company in Mobile would get your clothes clean. Dr. Joseph Patt's Germicide Solution for Lockjaw promised relief to sufferers with the mange, exema, distemper, and sore mouths—if taken in time. These businesses, located on Royal Street, were photographed circa 1907. (Mobile County. Courtesy of the University of South Alabama Archives.)

Engelhart's in Cullman, photographed in 1910, was typical of the small restaurants and cafes that sprang up across Alabama to meet the needs of business people in the town and offer entertainment alternatives for couples and families. Many of these establishments were operated by women, especially widows, who were able to convert their domestic training into the basis for successful businesses. (Cullman County. ADAH.)

Left: In the 1920s, this group of five entrepreneurs established "King Joy," a Chinese restaurant in Birmingham. They were, left to right, Mansion Joe, Loo Choy, Mrs. Loo Choy, Loo Bing, and George Sai. (Jefferson County. Courtesy of Henry Joe.)

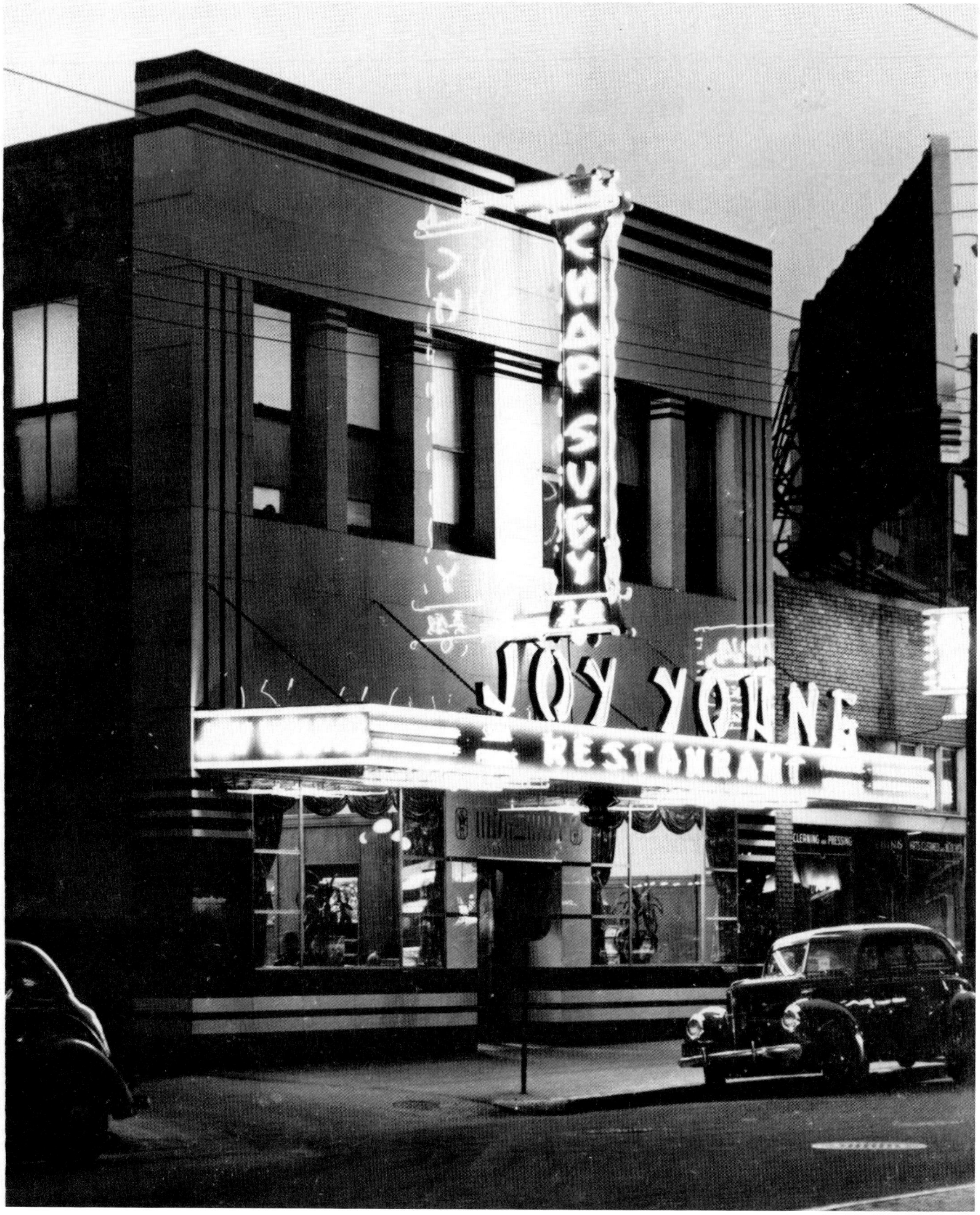
CHOP SUEY
JOY YOUNG
RESTAURANT
CLEANING AND PRESSING

Technology produced new jobs, such as those available to women as telephone operators. This unidentified operator at a cord board was representative of hundreds of other Alabama women who were the friendly voice behind every call, the central link in early telecommunications. (Courtesy of BellSouth.)

Left: In 1925, the King Joy restaurant moved to Twentieth Street across from the Tutwiler Hotel and was renamed the Joy Young. Members of the Ku Klux Klan visited the restaurant in the 1920s in opposition to "immigrants and foreigners." The effort at intimidation backfired, and the Joy Young remained arguably the most popular Birmingham restaurant with out-of-town guests at the Tutwiler, as well as with local residents. Three generations of the same family have operated the restaurant: Mansion Joe, his son Joe Wing Soo, and his grandson Henry Joe. In 1980, the restaurant moved from downtown Birmingham to a suburban shopping center. (Jefferson County. Courtesy of Henry Joe.)

The Alabama Penny Savings Bank was founded in 1895 in Birmingham by William R. Pettiford, minister of Birmingham's Sixteenth Street Baptist Church. The bank was the first black-run bank in Alabama. It exemplified the far-reaching leadership of African-American ministers and the role churches played in providing economic and social services not always adequately provided by white-owned businesses and organizations. (Jefferson County. Courtesy of the Birmingham Public Library Department of Archives and Manuscripts.)

A supreme moment! First it was curb service at the drug store. Later it was a basic serving method for drive-ins that sprang up as a result of Americans' love affair with the automobile. These women were served at Albright and Hall's Drug Store at Old Government and Grant Streets in Mobile in 1931. (Mobile County. Courtesy of the University of South Alabama Archives.)

Selma's businessmen and investors kept abreast of financial developments in New York at the Selma Stock Exchange. (Dallas County. Courtesy of the Old Depot Museum, Inc.)

A 1933 tornado caused widespread devastation in Helena. The Adjutant General's Office provided storm relief, and the Alabama National Guard was deployed to prevent looting. (Shelby County. ADAH.)

From the earliest days of Cahawba to the present, Alabama's many river towns have been subject to floods, such as this one in Selma. (Dallas County. Courtesy of the Old Depot Museum, Inc.)

Over the decades, the handiwork of man often has collided with the forces of nature, and the pace of urban growth has taxed municipal resources. The civic pride of Alabamians, however, has prevailed as citizens have worked to make their communities a reflection of their ideals and hopes for the future. In the 1930s, Civil Works Administration workers created this park in downtown Heflin as a place for rest and recreation for residents and visitors alike.(Cleburne County. ADAH.)

Twenty-one students attended the Hickory Grove School in Lowndes County in 1907. This photograph was taken at a time when the state was struggling to upgrade its public school system. The picture reveals two common educational problems across the state—inadequate facilities and mixing a variety of ages of students in a single school. In 1907, the state passed an act to assist in the construction and repair of country schools. The need for separate elementary and secondary schools was under consideration at the time. (Lowndes County. ADAH.)

# eight
*Education*

As important as politics, agriculture, and industry are, they represent only parts of the larger mosaic that forms Alabama history. Education is another significant piece. In Alabama, education began as a private effort. Shortly after Mobile was founded in 1702, the Catholic order of Jesuits established a school. The first nonsectarian school was taught by John Pierce in a log cabin on Lake Tensaw in 1799. The territorial legislature chartered Washington Academy at St. Stephens in 1811 and Green Academy at Huntsville in 1812, but these institutions had no tax support.

When Alabama became a state in 1819, the federal government set aside the sixteenth section of every township for public schools; however, the state had few common or public schools. In the antebellum period, most elementary and all secondary education was dispensed through private academies. In 1860 Alabama had 206 academies with 10,778 students. These schools were diverse in sponsorship—private, municipal, church, fraternal—but similar in that classes were held in primitive facilities and one teacher taught ungraded classes that were most often segregated by sex. Even so, several academies achieved academic distinction. Among them was Dr. Henry Tutwiler's Green Springs

Children played on the playground at Barker School in Birmingham circa 1913. This photograph is part of a collection of photographs and postcards collected by the Alabama Superintendent of Education. (Jefferson County. ADAH.)

By 1910, the Alabama Department of Education had become interested in the competent and systematic supervision of Negro rural schools in the state. Through grants from the General Education Board of the Rockefeller Foundation, state agents for Negro schools occupied positions as state superintendents to supervise state and philanthropic activities in this area. The General Education Board also helped extend a philanthropic program known as the Anna T. Jeanes–Negro Rural School Fund for the purpose of school supervision. The Jeanes workers oversaw primary instruction in the schools, organized industrial classes, and instructed in handicrafts, home industries, and homemaking. On July 26, 1915, one of these programs was held at a Eutaw church in Greene County. Thirty-eight teachers attended the workshop that featured grammar grade methods, gardening, sanitation, removal of illiteracy, sewing and cooking, games and songs, a canning demonstration, an exhibit of industrial arts, and a fireless cooker. In this photograph, one of the superintendents sat behind a display of canned items and close to an industrial arts exhibit. (Greene County. ADAH.)

On July 5, 1915, Dr. Booker T. Washington, president of Tuskegee Institute, participated in dedication services for the Coosa County Negro teacher training school at Cottage Grove. Nineteen teachers attended the training institute which stressed agriculture, sewing, and cobbling. The dedication ceremony, held at the close of the institute, attracted almost two thousand people. (Coosa County. ADAH.)

Many Alabama schools for black children taught skilled labor. In the early 1920s, young boys laid bricks for the new Calhoun County Training School which served the educational needs of Hobson City children. (Calhoun County. Courtesy of the Russell Collection, Public Library of Anniston and Calhoun County.)

The LaFayette High School in Chambers County was typical of early twentieth-century high schools in Alabama's larger towns. (Chambers County. Postcard from the collections of the ADAH.)

The Millerville School in Clay County was one of the first consolidated schools in Alabama. In 1920, the school bus, driven by Holloway Catchings, brought children from as far away as Shady Grove. (Clay County. Courtesy of the Auburn University Center for Arts and Humanities.)

Academy in Greene (now Hale) County, founded in 1847 and famous for its science curriculum.

The best education in the antebellum period was private education, and only a minority of white Alabamians could afford it. Consequently, many citizens, most of whom had grown up in frontier Alabama, had little formal education. Alabama's slave code prohibited teaching slaves to read and write.

Mobile took the early lead in public education. The city's Board of School Commissioners ordered construction of Barton Academy on Government Street and leased it to denominational and private schools. Then in 1852, Willis G. Clark organized Alabama's first public school system. Graded classes, emphasis on education, and some tax support made Mobile the exception to statewide conditions. In a predominantly rural, agricultural society, Alabamians in general did not accept the idea that public education was the responsibility of the taxpayers.

In 1854, Alexander B. Meek, a legislator from Mobile, wrote Alabama's first law providing for public education with a state superintendent of education elected by the legislature and an annual budget. William F. Perry was selected the first superintendent, and, in 1856, the Alabama Education Association was founded. Even with this initiative, however, the state did not provide consistent or

The people of Pinson in eastern Jefferson County met at the Baptist Church in the spring of 1921 to discuss how they might build a new school for their children. The county could not help, so the people collected donations, purchased land, and built this six-room schoolhouse themselves, using rocks which were common in the area. The school was completed in September 1922. Rock construction, almost a folk art, was also used for houses and stores. (Jefferson County. Courtesy of the Auburn University Archives.)

Below: With the consolidation movement, many rural schools combined, and school buses were used to transport students from homes distant from the schools. This 1928 Model A Ford bus was built by G. H. Brummel and used in Calhoun County. (Calhoun County. Courtesy of the Russell Collection, Public Library of Anniston and Calhoun County.)

*133*

This "homemade" school in Jackson County was typical of many rural schools in Alabama in the 1930s. Arthur Rothstein, a photographer with the Alabama Writers' Project, photographed the school at Skyline Farms in February 1937. The Skyline Farms Project was one of the most extensive projects of the federal Resettlement Administration. The Resettlement Administration was established in 1935 to provide rural rehabilitation by selling land to poor farmers and providing them with credit and assistance. Despite friction between the independent Appalachian farmers and federal bureaucrats, Skyline Farms promoted the appreciation and application of Appalachian folkways. Unfortunately, it was financially unsuccessful. (Jackson County. Courtesy of the Library of Congress.)

Until the 1960s, African-American schools were segregated and most often not of the same quality as white facilities. This is a class of first graders at Gee's Bend School in the 1930s. (Wilcox County. Courtesy of the Library of Congress.)

In 1933 and 1934, Civil Works Administration (CWA) projects provided important renovation and new construction for many Alabama schools. With this addition to Choctaw County High School in Butler, the CWA provided jobs for unemployed Alabamians at the same time it improved the educational environment for the state's young people. (Choctaw County. ADAH.)

The Barber Memorial Seminary was founded in 1896 in Anniston as a private school for African-American girls. Mrs. M. M. Barber of Philadelphia established the school as a memorial to her husband. The school, operated by the board of National Missions of the Presbyterian Church U.S.A., closed in 1942. (Calhoun County. Courtesy of the Russell Collection, Public Library of Anniston and Calhoun County.)

Right: Elementary schools were widespread across the state, but high school education was rare until the county consolidated high school program began after World War I. This kindergarten class in Eufaula was photographed in the 1930s as part of the Alabama Writers' Project. (Barbour County. ADAH.)

adequate public funding for education. In 1860 Alabama established a School for the Deaf and Dumb at Talladega under the leadership of Dr. Joseph Henry Johnson (the Blind School was added in 1867).

Although only a small percentage of Alabamians went to college before 1860, the state had a respectable number of institutions of higher learning. Most were private, church affiliated, more available to males than females, and emphasized the classics. Spring Hill in Mobile, which laid its cornerstone on July 4, 1830, is the state's oldest private college and the first permanent Catholic college in the South. The Baptists founded two colleges at Marion—The Judson Female Institute in 1839 and Howard College in 1841. The Methodists established La Grange College in 1830, Athens Female College in 1840, Southern University at Greensboro, and in 1856 the East Alabama Male College at Auburn and Tuskegee Female College, which later was moved to Montgomery and became Huntingdon College.

The University of Alabama, supported by initial federal land grants, was incorporated in 1819, but it was 1828 before the trustees chose Tuscaloosa as the site and construction was started. Thirty-five students began attending classes in 1831, even as buildings were being completed.

The Civil War crippled and closed schools, forcing a reevaluation and a reordering of education

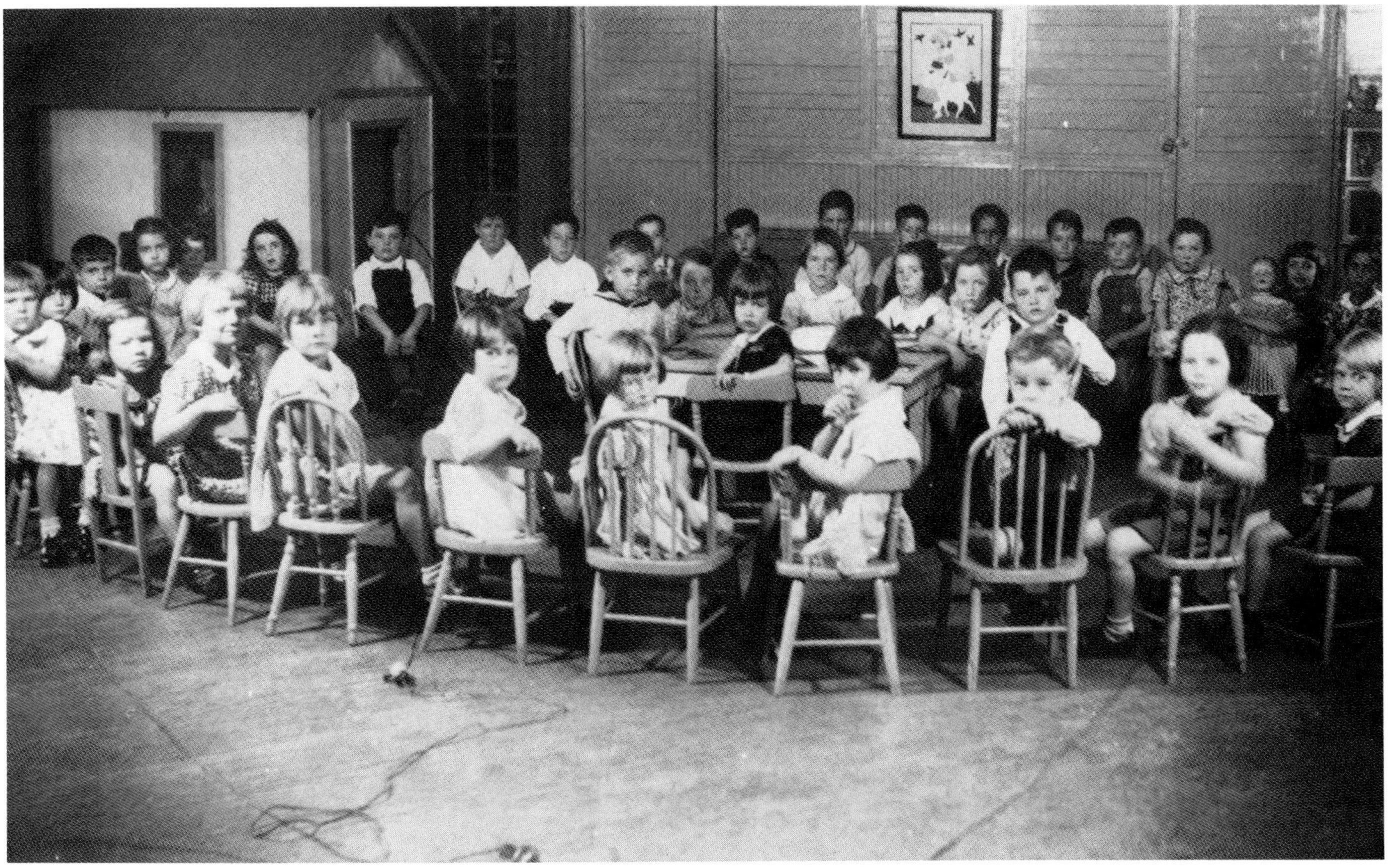

The Birmingham Public Library moved into a new building in 1927. (Jefferson County. ADAH.)

Small towns were pleased to have any library at all. This one in Point Clear was touted on a postcard as being the smallest library in the world. (Baldwin County. Courtesy of the University of South Alabama Archives.)

School libraries were important educational resources, but books were not plentiful. The Gadsden Public Library opened on May 13, 1938. Its children's room offered a sunny, inviting location for study and leisurely reading. (Etowah County. ADAH.)

Right: In rural areas, counties often operated trucks which brought books to citizens who could not travel to the library and which supplemented the meager libraries in local schools. In the 1920s, the Randolph County library truck called at a local school, which was dependent upon bookmobiles to provide reading materials to students. (Randolph County. ADAH.)

Spring Hill College in Mobile was founded by the Catholic church in 1830 and is the oldest college in Alabama. (Mobile County. Courtesy of the University of South Alabama Archives.)

during Reconstruction. The first provision for a true system of public education came in the Constitution of 1868, which mandated public education with "one or more schools in each district." Integrated schools were not required, but funds were divided almost equally between the races. Education, eagerly sought by former slaves, was augmented by many Northern teachers who came to the South and were funded by the Freedmen's Bureau or various northern churches and missionary societies.

After the Bourbon Democrats took control of state government, they wrote a new Alabama Constitution in 1875 and abolished many Republican agencies and policies. The new Constitution required separate schools for whites and blacks and severely limited state and county spending for education. School funding, never high on state government's agenda, was inadequate for both races. By 1891, when a law gave arbitrary power to township officials to apportion school funds, what was set aside for black schools and white schools lost all semblance of fairness.

Despite the work of educational leaders, the Constitution adopted in 1901 made few improvements in public education. Yet, remarkably, some progress was made. Early in the twentieth century, the legislature created a textbook commission, fixed minimum lengths for school terms, and appropriated more money. In the 1920s, Governor Bibb Graves achieved a minimum educational program for every county and created a state equalization fund to support the minimum program. Consolidation of schools and improved roads and highways helped make new educational opportunities more widely accessible.

After World War II, efforts by Alabama to preserve segregated schools by upgrading black education were cut short by the Supreme Court's

The Alabama Normal School was founded at Livingston in 1883, and Julia Tutwiler served as the school's principal. The school brought higher education close to young women in west Alabama. (Sumter County. Postcard from the collections of the ADAH.)

Troy State Normal College was one of four colleges Alabama founded to educate teachers. This photograph was taken during the 1899–1900 term. (Pike County. ADAH.)

Left: Tuskegee Institute, founded by Booker T. Washington, began with an emphasis upon industrial and occupational training, as in this class in the electrical shop. In addition, the college also had a fine liberal arts program, which turned out such noted writers as Harlem Renaissance novelist George Wylie Henderson. Henderson's first novel, *Ollie Miss*, was set in rural Macon County and was essentially a story of his mother. (Macon County. ADAH.)

This Smith–Hughes senior level class at Tuskegee Institute in 1917–1918 studied agriculture and methods of teaching. (Macon County. ADAH.)

Students at the State Normal School at Jacksonville refurbished their classroom equipment. In 1929, the school became Jacksonville State Teachers College. By 1957, it was Jacksonville State College, and, finally, in 1966 it was designated Jacksonville State University. (Calhoun County. ADAH.)

decision in 1954 that separate schools were unconstitutional. White citizens employed various legal strategies in efforts to resist compliance with the federal law, but, in September 1963, Alabama desegregated secondary schools for the first time.

Higher education after the Civil War went through periods of financial stringency. The University of Alabama had a difficult time during Reconstruction but managed to survive, in part because of talented and selfless faculty members. In 1872, a law school was established. In the twentieth century, extension divisions that evolved into degree-granting branch campuses were created by the University of Alabama at Birmingham, which became world famous for its medical and dental programs, and at Huntsville.

Private colleges continued after the war, but the major growth was in state-supported institutions. The need to train teachers led to the creation of several "normal" schools or teachers' colleges. The first such college was established in Florence in 1872. In 1974 this became the University of North Alabama. Other normal schools for whites were founded at Livingston, Jacksonville, and Troy.

In 1873, normal schools for blacks were established at Marion and Huntsville. The school at Marion evolved into Alabama State University at Montgomery, and, in the 1890s, the Huntsville school became Alabama's agricultural and mechanical college for blacks. Talladega College was a private school founded in 1865 by former slaves William Savery and Thomas Tarrant with help from the American Missionary Association.

In 1881, Booker T. Washington, who was born a slave in Virginia, was chosen principal and later president of Tuskegee Institute. The school at Tuskegee stressed vocational and industrial training and had on its faculty the scientist George

Auburn, the state's white land grant institution, offered scientific education with emphasis upon engineering and agriculture. Here cadets worked in the chemistry laboratory in 1893. (Lee County. Courtesy of the Auburn University Archives.)

Below: The Alabama Girls Industrial School opened as the state's first technical school for women on October 12, 1896. In 1911 the name of the school was changed to the Alabama Girls Technical Institute and, in 1919, to the Alabama Girls Technical Institute and College for Women to more accurately reflect its mission. Expanded programs led to further name changes: in 1923 to Alabama College, State College for Women and in 1956 to Alabama College when the school became co-educational. Finally, in 1969, the school's public liberal arts mission was reflected in the change to the University of Montevallo. This photograph of the library and main dormitory was made in the 1940s. (Shelby County. ADAH.)

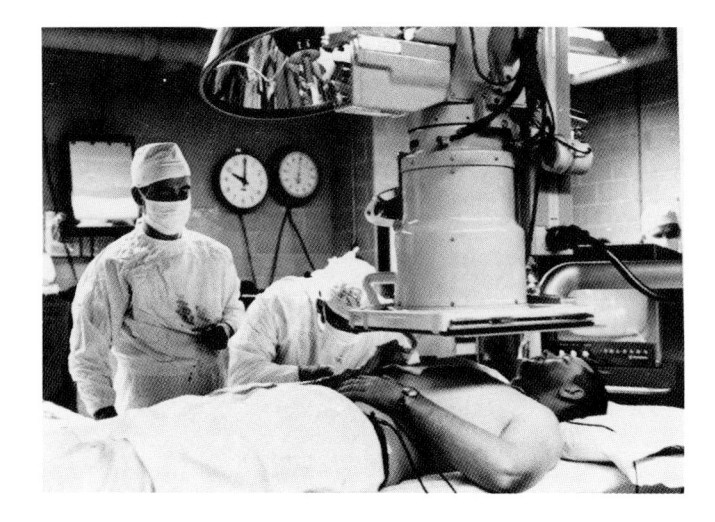

The University of Alabama at Birmingham (UAB) has gained an international reputation for its medical school. In 1993, UAB ranked in the top forty among American universities in acquiring federal research funds and was ranked twentieth in funding from the National Institutes of Health. By 1990, it had become the largest single employer in the Birmingham area. (Jefferson County. ADAH.)

Right: Denny Chimes is a campus landmark at the University of Alabama in Tuscaloosa. The chimes are named for George H. Denny who served as president of the University from 1912 to 1936 and then again for less than a year in 1941 after his successor died in office. During his tenure, Dr. Denny presided over remarkable growth in the physical facilities of the University, encouraged the enrollment of women, and maintained the school's financial well-being during the Depression years. The idea for the chimes was first raised in 1919 as a World War memorial and then resurrected in 1928 when rumors circulated that Dr. Denny was considering returning to Washington and Lee University. The chimes were built largely with funds raised by students and dedicated in 1929. (Tuscaloosa County. Courtesy of the William Stanley Hoole Special Collections Library, University of Alabama.)

Washington Carver and the man who pioneered agricultural extension work for blacks, Thomas Monroe Campbell.

Although the East Alabama Male College at Auburn opened before the Civil War, the small Methodist liberal arts college could not survive the postwar period and was given to the state in 1872 to become the Alabama Agricultural and Mechanical College. As the land-grant college for whites, Auburn educated engineers and scientifically trained agricultural teachers and researchers. The school took a pioneering step when it admitted women in 1892, and, in 1899, with its new name, Alabama Polytechnic Institute, continued its mission. In 1960, its name was changed to Auburn University, and a branch campus at Montgomery was opened in 1968.

In 1892, the state legislature authorized the Alabama Girls Industrial School at Montevallo, a centrally located institution that began accepting students in 1896 and became the University of Montevallo in 1969. The University of South Alabama opened in 1964 and has grown rapidly and provided a second medical school for the state. Under Governor George C. Wallace, the Alabama Trade School and Junior College Authority was created, which established a number of schools with emphasis upon affordable tuition and geographical balance.

Although Alabama was slow in developing educational opportunities for its citizens and has not always funded these schools adequately, by the end of the twentieth century an extensive network of state-supported technical schools, junior colleges, and universities, including a law school and two medical schools, made higher education readily accessible to all Alabama citizens.

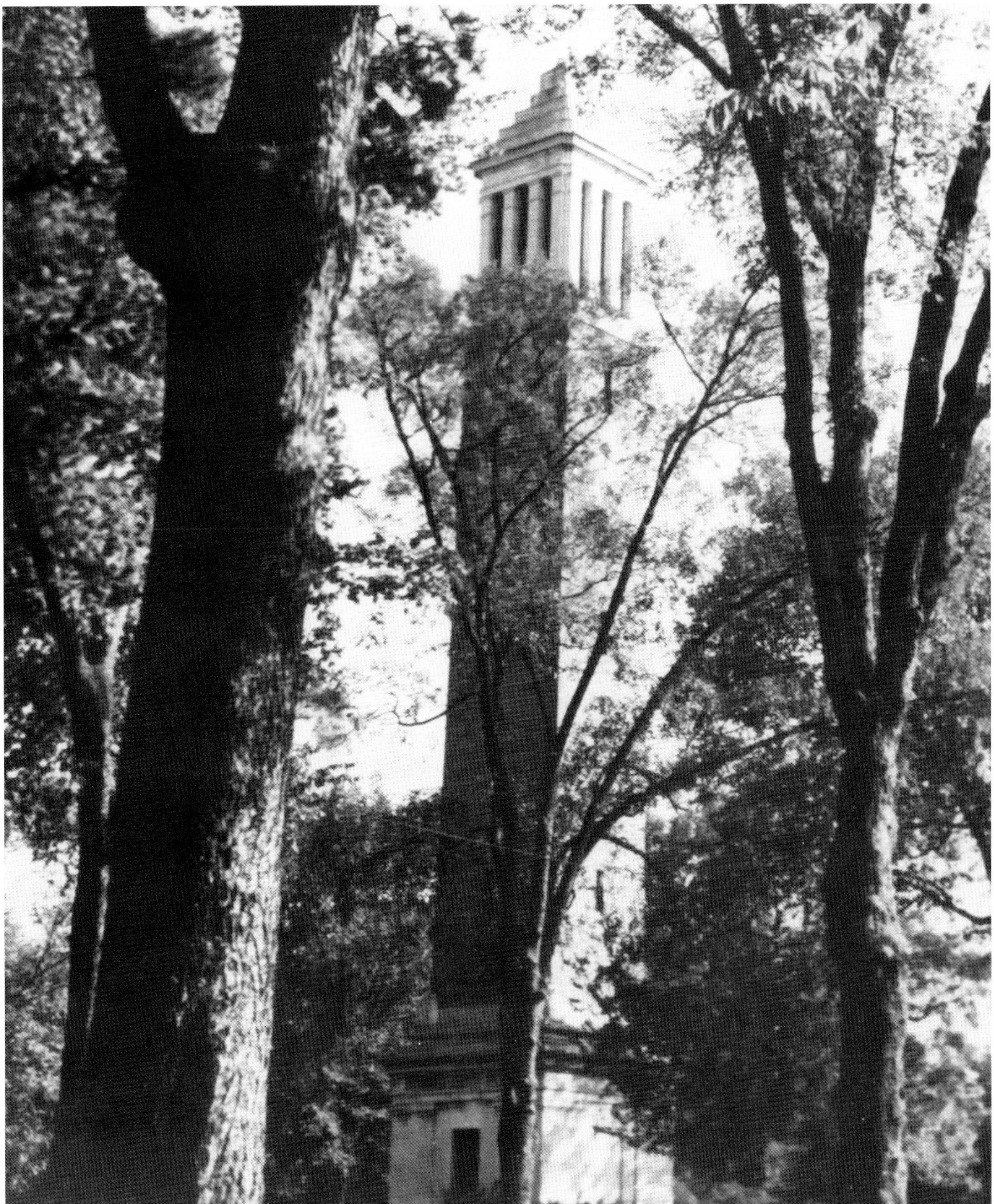

Since the founding of the state, religion has been the foundation for Alabama families. This woman, identified only as Aunt Matt, was photographed in Crenshaw County circa 1890 with two young children by her side and the Bible in her lap. (Crenshaw County. ADAH.)

# nine
*Religion*

Religion is an important part of the lives of Alabama citizens, and it has helped shape the state's culture in many ways. French Catholics brought Christianity to Alabama when they arrived in 1702, and the church was strengthened when Spain controlled Mobile between 1780 and 1813. The port city also was the point of entry for many Jews coming to Alabama in the antebellum period. Yet most Alabamians, true to the heritage of the early settlers from the Eastern Seaboard states and Tennessee, were Protestants. In the twentieth century, the increased fragmentation of Protestant denominations and the introduction of new religions from Greek Orthodox to Islam and Buddhism have brought greater diversity of religion to Alabama.

In the antebellum period, whites supervised the slaves' religion, which was mainly Protestant but much influenced by their African heritage. Slaves attended and were members of some churches and were preached to by white ministers. If a black minister delivered a sermon, it was supposed to be under white supervision, but often there were secret services in wooded areas of plantations.

During Reconstruction, blacks quickly established separate denominations such as the Baptist, African Methodist Episcopal Zion, and the African Methodist

The only identification for this photograph is "Lambert's S. S. Class." Mr. Lambert stood at the back of the group, and J. P. Roberts stood on the right for this picture. Classes such as these have met across Alabama every Sunday morning for generations. (ADAH.)

By the beginning of the twentieth century, Alabama was overwhelmingly Protestant with Baptists and Methodists almost equal in strength. In the next few decades, the Baptist Church pulled ahead to become the largest denomination in the state. The church required total immersion baptisms, and baptisms, like this one in the 1920s, were special events that often drew large crowds. This congregation gathered on the banks of the Tennessee River in Decatur in 1905. (Morgan County. Courtesy of the Wheeler Basin Regional Library.)

Gee's Bend, nestled in a large bulb-shaped curve in the Alabama River in Wilcox County, is almost surrounded by water. Named for the planter who settled there with his slaves early in the nineteenth century, many of the Bend's freed blacks remained on the land as tenants after the Civil War and developed an independence and a culture so distinctive that other blacks in the area called them "Africans." Religion is an important part of the culture and outdoor baptisms significant events. In this circa 1990 photograph, church members, families, and friends gathered to witness the immersion of new Christians, who are standing behind the minister dressed in white with their heads tied in white scarves. (Wilcox County. Courtesy of the Birmingham Public Library Department of Archives and Manuscripts.)

Montgomery photographer Stanley Paulger photographed the 1929 Confirmation Class of Temple Beth-Or. Rabbi William B. Schwartz stood in the center of the group in a dark suit. The Temple, located at the corner of Clayton and Sayre Streets, was built in 1901. (Montgomery County. Courtesy of Cecelia Zimmerman.)

Funerals are times for families to gather to mourn the dead and renew family bonds. Relatives of Lemuel Jordan, who died November 21, 1938, gathered at his graveside in Lambeth Free Holiness Cemetery for several snapshots that documented the generations of the family. In this picture, Jordan's three sons stood by their father's grave. (Escambia County. Courtesy of Robert Bradley.)

Marshall Rhodes and his second wife were married in Barbour County in the 1930s in front of a large crowd of relatives and friends. Rhodes had seven children by his first marriage, and she had six. The two young women on the far left and far right in the front row served as bridesmaids. (Barbour County. ADAH.)

Right: Clarence and Katherine Ruputha Brunner commemorated their First Communion in the St. John's Lutheran Church with this photograph taken around 1910. (Cullman County. Courtesy of Rickie Louise Brunner.)

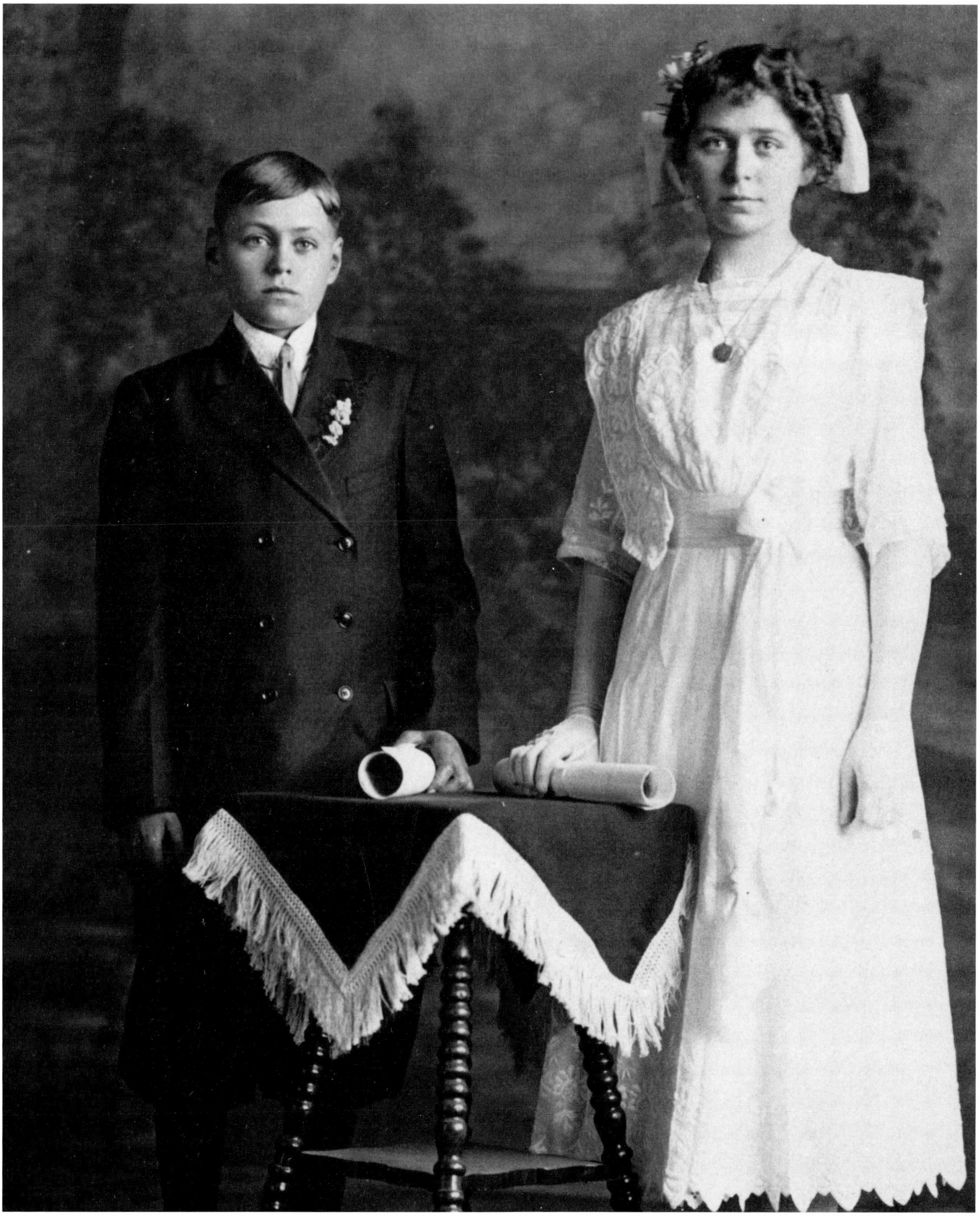

The Sixteenth Street Baptist Church, founded in 1873, was the first black church in downtown Birmingham. The church served middle- and upper-class professional blacks, and its ministers took a leadership role in the community. The choir posed in 1918 on the front steps where forty-five years later a bomb was placed that killed four young girls. (Jefferson County. Courtesy of the Birmingham Public Library Department of Archives and Manuscripts.)

Episcopal. The church, as a segregated but independent institution, became a powerful force in black society.

In Alabama, ministers, both black and white, historically have been influential members of their communities. Frequently, but with certain exceptions, Southern white churches have emphasized personal conduct and individual salvation rather than social issues such as race relations, child labor, women's rights, and prison conditions. Black churches, while often equally strong in their emphasis on personal salvation, have particularly been centers of leadership in social action.

In the 1950s and 1960s, Southern churches and ministers, especially black denominations and leaders but some white preachers as well, joined the surging vanguard of the movement to secure civil rights for blacks. The use of moral precepts to obtain political ends was brought to bear with compelling logic. The rhetoric of religious sentiment proved effective in the fight for political equality. Black ministers Ralph D. Abernathy of Montgomery, Fred L. Shuttlesworth Jr. of Birmingham, and Joseph E. Lowry of Mobile, along with the Reverend Martin Luther King Jr., helped give a religious base to the movement for profound societal change.

The time of the civil rights movement was one of turmoil and struggle—from the Montgomery bus boycott in 1955–1956, to the freedom riders and marchers, to school integration at every level, to voting rights. During the movement, religion was a philosophical, theological, and pragmatic buttress for black Alabamians as they struggled to enjoy the promises of democracy.

The church has always been a place where individuals declare their belief or have their faith renewed. Some people are christened in churches,

Left: Within black society, the church was not only a religious institution but also was responsible for social activities and leadership training for the African-American community. Thankful Church, Hoboken, in Eufaula reflects life in many other black churches in the mid-twentieth century. (Barbour County. ADAH.)

Below: The rural areas of Alabama always have been strong centers of evangelical Christianity. Richard Rose McAdory led his Sunday school class at the Pleasant Hill Methodist Church in western Jefferson County during the late 1920s. This scene was typical of Sunday morning activities across the state. (Jefferson County. Courtesy of Henry and Betty McAdory.)

baptized in them, or married in them. Dignified and formal last respects are often paid in churches. Churches are also social centers and places for "dressing up" or dinners on the ground. And a church is a place to sing. Alabamians have always enjoyed affirming that they are both "Standing on the Promises" and "Leaning on the Everlasting Arms." Rural revivals in Macon County or Lamar County or in any one of the state's sixty-seven counties have the common goal of adding members and saving souls. Each one has its own unique aura, in part as a community experience and in part as an expression of higher beliefs that transcend the immediate world of the believers.

During the 1930s, many churches sponsored Tom Thumb weddings where children dressed up like adults and pretended to marry. This "wedding" was held at the First Methodist Church in Sylacauga in 1933. (Talladega County. Courtesy of the B. B. Comer Memorial Library.)

Revivals were important religious and social occasions across Alabama in the late-nineteenth and early-twentieth centuries. This tent revival was held circa 1925 at the Fairmont Baptist Church in Red Level. (Covington County. Courtesy of Special Collection, Samford University Library)

Dinner on the grounds following Sunday services at this Primitive Baptist church in Monroe County in the 1950s followed a decades-old tradition. The dinner provided a time to socialize, allowed the women the opportunity to show off their cooking skills, and let everyone enjoy the best of Alabama food. (Monroe County. Photograph by Max McAliley. Courtesy of the Monroe Public Library.)

Bishop Richard Hooker Wilmer was the leader of the Episcopal Diocese of Alabama for thirty-eight years. He came to Alabama in 1862 as the only bishop consecrated by the Southern church after its secession from the national body. Wilmer became known as the "Confederate Bishop" after the Civil War for his order to suspend prayers in the churches for all civil authorities, including the president, until military rule was ended and civil authority restored to the state. As a result of Wilmer's stand, the churches were closed for about four months by Federal occupation troops, and it took a personal meeting between Bishop Wilmer and President Andrew Johnson to resolve the issue. (ADAH.)

By 1860 there were three Jewish congregations in Alabama, and the center of antebellum Jewish life was Mobile. By the end of the 1860's Jewish settlers had begun moving upriver to smaller communities, including Demopolis, Selma, Montgomery, Uniontown, and Eufaula. In the twentieth century, Jews in Alabama have tended to move to the larger cities, and congregations in the smaller communities have ceased to be the vital forces they once were. Rabbi Morris Newfield of Birmingham served as a part-time chaplain at Camp McClellan in Anniston during World War I. (Calhoun County. Courtesy of the Birmingham Public Library Department of Archives and Manuscripts.)

Many adults who did not have the opportunity to attend school as children began classes as adults to learn to read and write. Rural churches often served as educational centers, as well as the spiritual focus of the community. In the 1930s, this church in Gee's Bend was the site of adult education classes in basic reading, mathematical, and writing skills. (Wilcox County. Courtesy of the Library of Congress.)

Below: In 1908, Montgomery photographer Herbert P. Tresslar photographed the Salvation Army's second annual Fresh Air Encampment. A year earlier, this unique program had been started by Captain and Mrs. L. A. Odom to provide summer outings for "worthy persons" unable to afford them. The camp, located at Pickett Springs, provided free two-week vacations for some 350 people, primarily working women and children. (Montgomery County. ADAH.)

The Holt Street Baptist Church in Montgomery was the site of the first mass meeting on the Montgomery Bus Boycott. On the night of December 5, 1955, about five thousand black Montgomerians met in and around the church in support of the day-old boycott. For many, this was the first opportunity to hear Dr. Martin Luther King Jr. speak. (Montgomery County. Courtesy of the *Montgomery Advertiser*.)

Many recreational activities, like fishing, provide opportunities for generations to enjoy their leisure time together. In this picture circa 1950, two generations inspected the results of their fishing trip on the Coosa River. (Tallapoosa County. ADAH.)

# ten
*Leisure*

Fried chicken may reign supreme at church dinners on the grounds, but of course Alabamians do not wait for religious events to exercise their historic love of eating Southern delicacies: butter beans; field peas; fried and boiled okra; sweet potatoes, baked or in a soufflé; turnip greens, mustard greens, and collards; onions and squash; corn, on the cob or creamed; biscuits and corn bread; grits; pecan pie; and sweet iced tea. The attraction of traditional Southern dishes cuts across lines of race, age, sex, size, personality, and economic status. Alabamians not only love food, they think about it and talk about it. For them, eating may not be quite a sacred ritual, but it is close.

Eating is but one way Alabamians enjoy their leisure time. Throughout history, Alabamians have found much of their lives driven by events and forces beyond their control; however, within the limitations of their environment, time, and income, the state's citizens have always cherished their leisure.

Blessed with forests, fields, mountains, swamps, rivers, ponds, and lakes, Alabamians throughout history have indulged themselves in the pleasures of the outdoors. Like other Southerners, Alabamians love hunting and fishing. For many, the challenge of the hunt remains mythic and timeless, and the hours

Left: This group of youngsters, circa 1910, enjoyed the age-old game of jumping rope. (Macon County. ADAH.)

Governor Chauncey Sparks, who served from 1943 until 1947, participated in a hunt at the Bull Pen Hunting Club in the fall of 1945. (Washington County. Courtesy of Kathryn Tucker Windham.)

F. A. Mahan hit a drive in an 1890 golf game at the Montgomery Country Club. With him were Hardwick Ruth on his far right and G. W. Craik, the unidentified caddie, J. R. Sayre, and J. P. O'Connor to his left. (Montgomery County. ADAH.)

Since the earliest inhabitants, Alabamians have fished. Men, women, and children have fished the streams, lakes, rivers, and Gulf shores of Alabama both for sustenance and recreation. This man enjoyed a day of fishing at the "old gin" on Cypress Creek. (Lauderdale County. ADAH.)

*161*

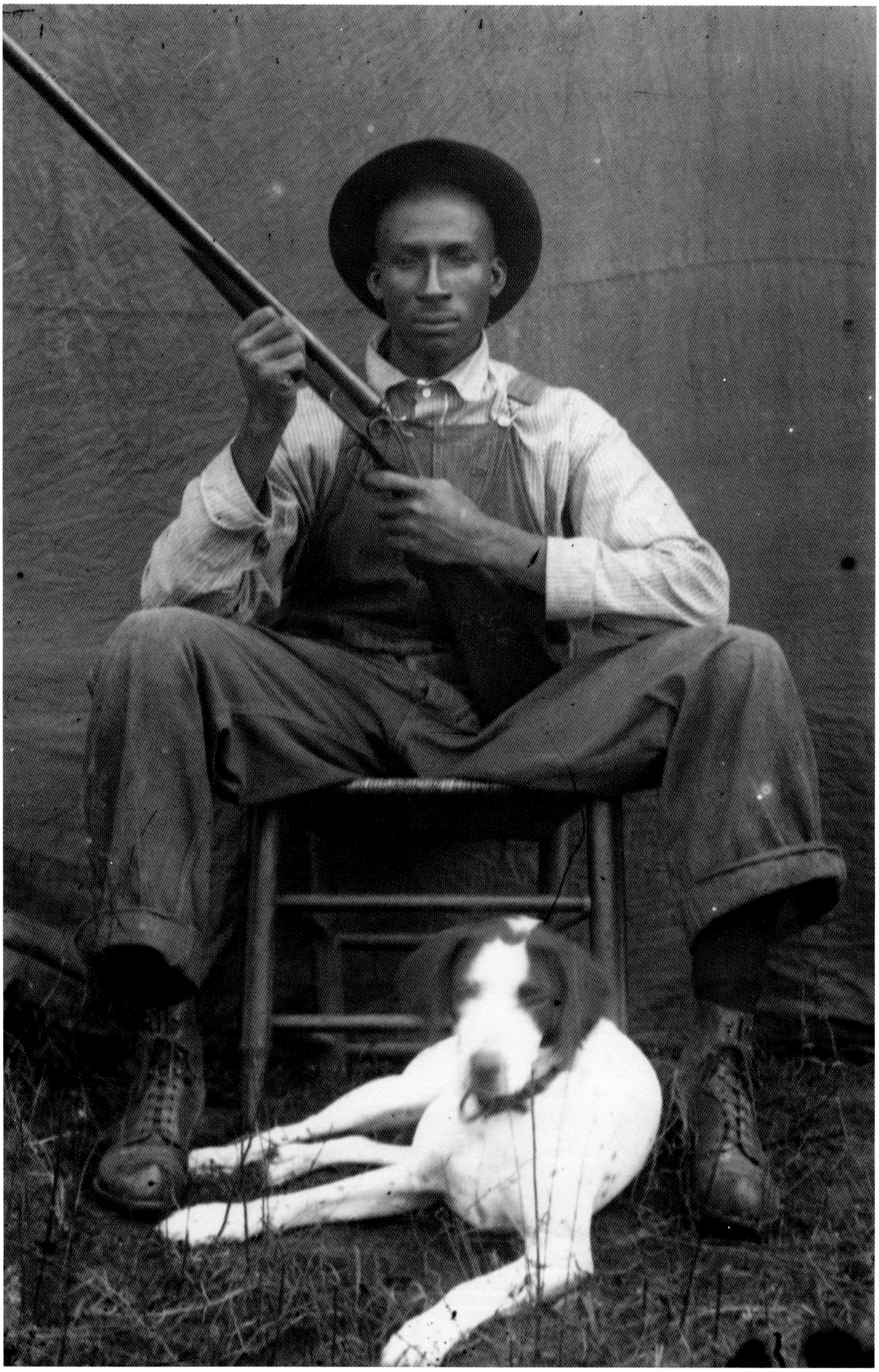

Organized team sports for girls were not as common as those for boys, but many city schools sponsored girls' basketball teams. Usually the girls' team played only intramurally, as this interclass championship team did in 1909. (Jefferson County. Courtesy of Leah Rawls Atkins.)

Millerville High School fielded this basketball team in 1924. By this time, the sport was popular and enabled small schools without the manpower or resources to field football teams to compete against each other. This team played twenty-two games without losing a single one. (Clay County. Courtesy of the Auburn University Center for the Arts and Humanities.)

The hunter, weapon, and dog are the classic components of a hunt. This hunter, circa 1915, may have been on a long hunt as indicated by the tent and chair. (Pike County. Courtesy of the University of South Alabama Archives.)

Baseball attracted interest at all levels, including this team that competed in the Fairfield Sheet Metal Industrial League. Just as today, most teams had bat boys who proudly performed their duties. (Jefferson County. Courtesy of the Birmingham Public Library Department of Archives and Manuscripts.)

by a lake or river a time of release and pleasure.

Competitive sports—whether individual or team, participatory or spectator, amateur or professional—are monumentally important in Alabama. Indeed, many rank the day of the annual Auburn-Alabama football game one of the single most important days of the year. Baseball is especially popular, and the state has produced such stars as Willie Mays, Hank Aaron, Dixie Walker, and many others. Jesse Owens won Olympic track medals and world fame in 1936 at the Berlin games, and Jennifer Chandler received a gold medal in diving at the 1976 Montreal Olympic games. Alabamians continue to distinguish themselves in all types of sports.

Alabamians play games, make music, enjoy solitude, engage in sports, express themselves through art and writing, go to dances, parties, and the movies, take excursions, join organizations, and pass traditional crafts down from generation to generation. Alabamians play out their leisure time in a broad range of activities that bring personal satisfaction and pleasure and add meaning to individual lives. These activities are inseparable from life in Alabama—past and present.

The Birmingham Black Barons was a team in the all-black professional baseball league. Black Barons' games at Rickwood Field attracted large crowds of both black and white baseball enthusiasts. Willie Mays began his outstanding career with the Birmingham team and went on to play in the major leagues after baseball was integrated in the late 1940s. In this photograph, Mays, at the top center, celebrated with his team mates in 1948. (Jefferson County. Courtesy of the *Birmingham World* Newspaper.)

Below: By the end of the nineteenth century, football was well established and popular. Rules and equipment changed over the years, but determination for victory was constant. The Marion Institute football team was state champion in 1912. (Perry County. ADAH.)

165

The University of Alabama football team competed against the University of Washington Huskies in the 1926 Rose Bowl game. The game was the first time a Southern team had competed in the Rose Bowl, and the invitation was issued only after several other schools had declined. The game carried such statewide significance that Alabamians gathered in theaters, auditoriums, and on the streets that New Year's Day to follow the account sent over a special Associated Press telegraph wire. The Alabama team, quarterbacked by Pooley Hubert and sparked by halfback Johnny Mack Brown, came back to score a 20–19 upset win. Victory celebrations filled the streets in Tuscaloosa, Birmingham, and Montgomery. The victory somehow seemed to carry a significance far beyond just winning a game. The *Atlanta Georgian* newspaper called the win "the greatest victory for the South since the first battle of Bull Run." Andy Doyle, an adjunct faculty member at Auburn University in Montgomery, has written: "It evoked the timeless spirit of the Lost Cause while it embodied the competitive self-confidence so vital to 20th century capitalism." Doyle cites John Temple Graves, a Birmingham newspaper editor, who in 1941 reflected on the 1926 and 1927 Rose Bowl victories: "For all the last stands, all the lost causes and sacrificings in vain, the South had a heart. And a tradition. But the South had a new tradition for something else. It was for survival, and for victory. It had come from the football fields. It had come from those mighty afternoons in the Rose Bowl at Pasadena, when Alabama's Crimson Tide had rolled to glory. . . . The South had come by way of football to think at last in terms of causes won, not lost." (Pasadena, Ca. Courtesy of the Paul W. Bryant Museum, University of Alabama.)

Right: Three players on Mobile's Dunbar High School football team posed for the camera in 1946. (Mobile County. Courtesy of the University of South Alabama Archives.)

In December 1873, the state legislature created two black normal schools. The Huntsville Normal and Industrial School opened in 1875 and was the genesis for what is now Alabama Agricultural and Mechanical University in Normal. The normal school and university at Marion was established to provide "for the liberal education of the colored race." In 1889, the school was renamed the State Normal School for Colored Students and relocated to Montgomery. As the school evolved, it went through several name changes to reflect its growth: from State Teachers College to Alabama State College for Negroes and then to Alabama State College. In 1969, the school was designated Alabama State University. In 1924, Cliff Green and Fred Cramton, two white Montgomerians who were close friends and avid football fans, came together to organize and promote what has become the country's oldest black college football classic, the annual Thanksgiving Day game between Alabama State University and Tuskegee University. Although segregation was a fact of Southern life in the first decades of the twentieth century, the game drew large numbers of both black and white fans—over eight thousand attended the first game. This photograph records a parade in downtown Montgomery, circa 1946, for what was originally named the Annual "Cramton Bowl" Dixie Classic. Now called the Turkey Day Classic, the game is still a major sports event for fans and alumni alike. (Montgomery County. ADAH.)

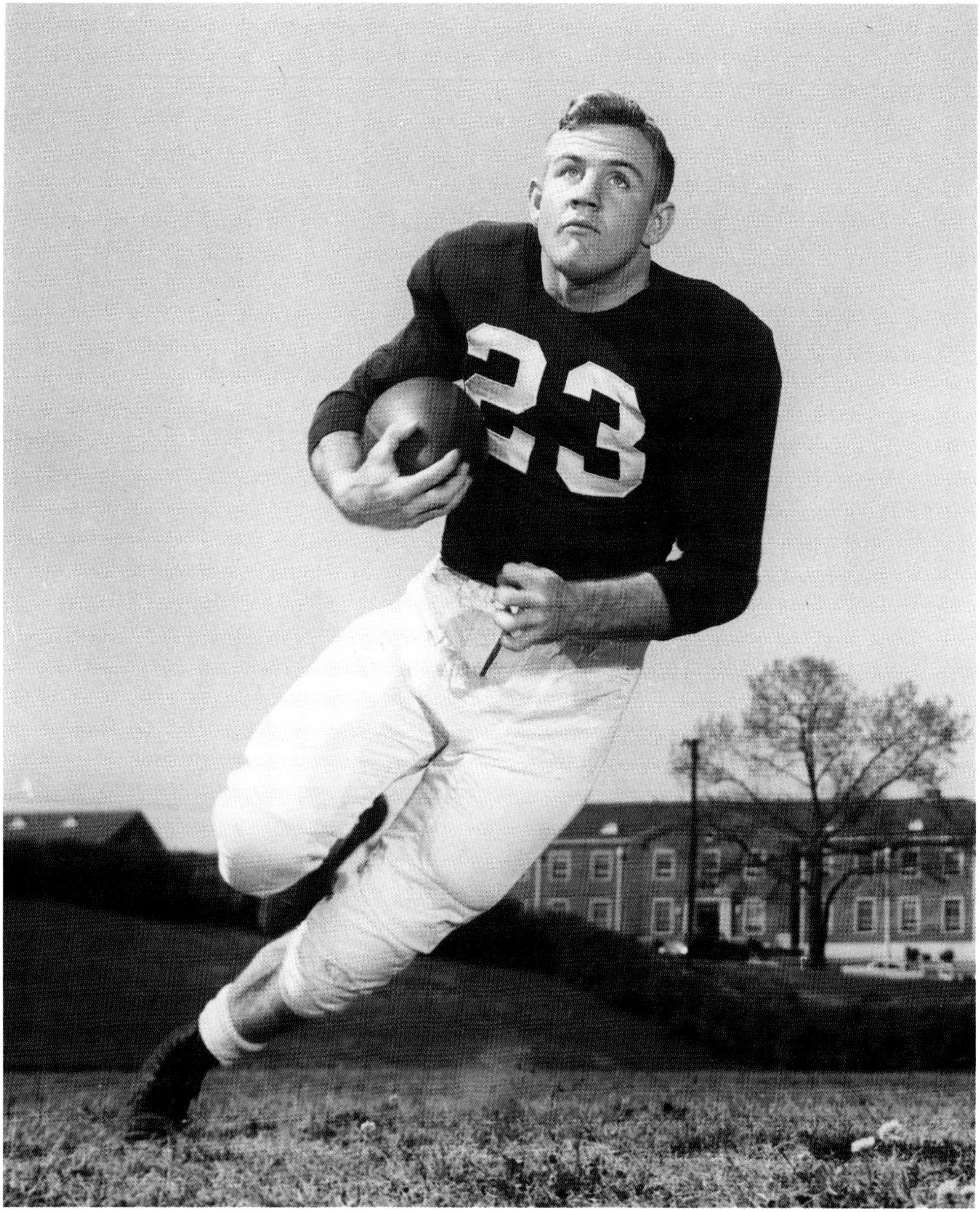
23

Left: Auburn University's football tradition began in 1891 when Dr. George Petrie, a professor of history and Latin fresh from Johns Hopkins University in Baltimore, volunteered to teach interested Alabama Agricultural and Mechanical College students to play "scientific football," as distinguished from soccer. In 1892, Auburn played—and won—its first game by defeating the University of Georgia 10–0 at a game in Atlanta. Some sixty years later, Forrest "Fob" James Jr., a native of Lee County, was a star fullback on the Auburn University football squad from 1953 to 1955 and was named All-American in 1955. A civil engineering graduate, James worked with the state highway department for several years before founding his own sports equipment manufacturing company. He was elected governor of Alabama as a Democrat in 1978 but chose not to run for a second term. He later reentered politics as a Republican and was elected governor again in 1994. (Lee County. Courtesy of the Auburn University Photographic Services.)

Football, politics, and industrial development met in Birmingham on October 16, 1993. From left to right, Dr. Roger Sayers, president of the University of Alabama, Governor Jim Folsom, and Andreas Renschler, president of Mercedes-Benz of Alabama, celebrated after the Mercedes-Benz logo was unveiled atop the scoreboards at Legion Field before the Alabama-Tennessee game. (Jefferson County. ADAH.)

Paul "Bear" Bryant, legendary head football coach at the University of Alabama, met rival Auburn University coach Ralph "Shug" Jordan at Legion Field in Birmingham following the famous 1972 game which Auburn won 17–16 after blocking two Alabama punts and recovering them in the end zone for touchdowns. (Jefferson County. Courtesy of Auburn University Photographic Services.)

Rodeos, such as those held annually by the Alabama Cattlemen's Association, are popular forms of entertainment. This rodeo, held in Montgomery circa 1950, reflected a resurgence of the cattle industry in Alabama in the mid-twentieth century. (Montgomery County. ADAH.)

Vulcan, Roman god of fire and metal working, came to symbolize Birmingham's leadership in the iron and steel industry. Vulcan originally was built as Birmingham's entry into the 1904 St. Louis Exposition. Frederick M. Jackson Sr., president of the Birmingham Commercial Club, spearheaded the drive to raise funds for the statue which was created by sculptor Giuseppe Moretti. When completed, the statue stood fifty-six feet tall and weighed approximately 120,000 pounds. After the statue's triumphant return to Birmingham, problems with funding and finding a proper location tarnished Vulcan's image. Finally, a location at the state fairground was offered, and Vulcan remained there for nearly thirty years—unable to hold his spear or hammer because both his right hand and left arm were improperly installed. At this mid-1930s Alabama state fair, the statue stood between the Industrial Arts Building and the main dining hall, close to the paddock and race track. Ultimately, U.S. Steel donated a permanent home for Vulcan, and the Works Progress Administration funded construction of Vulcan Park. By 1939, Vulcan was installed in his present location overlooking the Magic City from atop Red Mountain. (Jefferson County. Courtesy of the Birmingham Public Library Department of Archives and Manuscripts.)

Right: The Rattlesnake Rodeo, sponsored by the Opp Jaycees, is an annual festival in South Alabama. Auston Davis, an expert handler, wore a snakeskin vest while handling a big rattler at the 1981 Rodeo. (Covington County. Courtesy of the Opp Public Library.)

*170*

This flower-bedecked carriage was part of the Fourth of July parade in Huntsville in 1899. Pictured are Sarah Dement and Mamie Fletcher with Robert Weeden and Hector Lane. (Madison County. ADAH.)

A large crowd viewed a regatta on Guntersville Lake on August 6, 1939. One observer estimated the throng at seventy-five thousand. (Marshall County. ADAH.)

This Christmas party was given in 1915 for the children of families working in the ore mines of the Ishkooda Division of the Tennessee Coal, Iron and Railroad Company. (Jefferson County. Courtesy of Special Collection, Samford University Library.)

Right: Mobile's celebration of Mardi Gras began in 1868, but the roots of Mardi Gras itself can be traced back to the sixteenth century. The pre-Lenten carnival climaxes on Shrove Tuesday and, while Catholic in origin, it has become a major social event for Alabamians of all persuasions. It reflects the Gulf area's French and Spanish influence. In this parade in the 1940s, floats relied on mule power. (Mobile County. Courtesy of the University of South Alabama Archives.)

Each Alabama family has its individual traditions and rituals, many of which revolve around holidays and special occasions. Christmas Day in the Engelhardt home in Montgomery in 1921 was documented by photographer John E. Scott Sr. Clara Elizabeth and John Engelhardt Jr. posed under the Christmas tree with their new toys. (Montgomery County. Courtesy of Robert Fouts.)

The Fairhope Single Tax Colony was established in 1894 when several families moved to Alabama from Iowa to establish a model community based on Henry George's theory of a single tax. Led by Ernest B. Gaston, colonists believed that the prevailing social and economic order was doomed and that land ownership promoted greed, ultimately leading to poverty for most people. Colony members did not own land but instead rented it for a single tax. The beachfront area on Mobile Bay was reserved for public recreational use. For years before the bridge and causeway were constructed, the quickest way to travel between Mobile and Fairhope was by passenger boat that ran a regular schedule across the Bay. The *Bay Queen* was popular with excursionists on Mobile Bay in the 1930s. (Baldwin County. Courtesy of the University of South Alabama Archives.)

Boys 4-H Clubs were both educational and social organizations. A group of young men from Macon County enjoyed Vaughan's Mill in August 1925. (Macon County. Courtesy of the Auburn University Archives.)

In the post–World War I era, bathing suits became increasingly practical although shoes and stockings still were considered a part of beachwear. Umbrellas gave protection from the sun and added an extra touch of femininity to this 1920s bathing beauty contest in South Alabama. (Courtesy of the University of South Alabama Archives.)

Driving to the Gulf and camping out on the beach was an inexpensive way for a family to vacation. Because of poor roads, nearly all of them unpaved, a trip from Central Alabama could take a full day. Extra tires and tubes were necessary because the driver could count on several flat tires along the way. (Courtesy of Flora Maye Simmons.)

This troop of Mobile Boy Scouts represented the strong scouting movement in Alabama. (Mobile County. Courtesy of the University of South Alabama Archives.)

Fraternal organizations became important social groups for men in the late nineteenth century. Both black and white organizations flourished in large and small communities across the state. Members of the Kennedy Lodge No. 302 of the International Order of Odd Fellows gathered in front of the Walker Hotel in Kennedy circa 1908. (Lamar County. Courtesy of Mickey Watkins.)

Music always has been a favorite way for Alabamians to express themselves. From mountain fiddling contests to marching brass bands, from traditional black spirituals to shape note singing, music brought a lift to the soul. Eugene Jordan Sr. led the Ozark City Band circa 1890. (Dale County. ADAH.)

Children always have enjoyed outdoor activities, even those as quiet as reading and storytelling. This photograph, circa 1890, may be of a Cumberland Presbyterian Church Sunday school class outing to Lake Rhea. (Etowah County. Courtesy of John McFarland.)

Fess Whatley, who taught music at Birmingham's Industrial High School (later Parker High School), is considered the father of jazz music in Birmingham. Many of Whatley's students went on to earn national reputations, playing in Hollywood and New York City. Whatley's own band, known in the 1920s as the Jazz Demons, introduced Birmingham to the sounds of the 1920s and was one of the most popular dance orchestras in the city. (Jefferson County. Courtesy of the Birmingham Public Library Department of Archives and Manuscripts.)

Old and new traditions collided in the 1930s as country farmers came to town to enjoy the music and spectacle of minstrel and vaudeville shows. Walker Evans took this photograph as part of his work documenting the programs of the federal Resettlement Administration. (Courtesy of the Library of Congress.)

The Auburn Knights were a popular college dance band that toured the state in the 1930s, playing for social functions and dances. Over the years, the Knights graduated some outstanding musicians, such as Toni Tenille, a vocalist who later had a television and recording career, Urbie Green, a trombonist featured in "The Benny Goodman Story", and Dave Edwards, a saxophonist in 1959–1960 who later played with the Lawrence Welk orchestra. (Lee County. Courtesy of the Auburn University Archives.)

During World War II, communities and youth service organizations hosted dances for local teenagers. This dance was held in Decatur. (Morgan County. ADAH.)

Left: Hank Williams, who was born in Mount Olive in Butler County in 1923, learned the blues from a black man in Georgiana. He began his country music career with a band that played in Montgomery and the honky-tonks around World War II Mobile. Williams became a star after he joined the Grand Ole Opry in 1949. His song lyrics touched the heart of postwar America, and his music combined both black and white musical traditions. Williams died on January 1, 1953, at the age of twenty-nine. On September 20–21, 1954, the Alcazar Shrine Temple in Montgomery hosted a Hank Williams Memorial celebration. As the *Montgomery Advertiser* noted, "Stars—hundreds of them—descended on Dexter Avenue yesterday to take part in a record breaking neon colored parade saluting the memory of Hank Williams." Roy Acuff hosted the event, and dozens of Nashville stars, among them Minnie Pearl and Kitty Wells, took part in the festivities that included an open-air show at Normandale for ten thousand people. During the celebration, the monument was unveiled that would stand over Williams' grave in Oakwood Cemetery Annex. The simple inscription reads: "Praise The Lord, I Saw The Light." A crowd of sixty thousand lined Dexter Avenue for a parade that featured Williams' family members including his mother, Mrs. Lillian Williams Stone, who rode in one of the Cadillacs that had belonged to Williams. (Montgomery County. ADAH.)

*177*

Thomas W. Hollingsworth, his wife, Mary E., and their children posed in a photographer's studio for this portrait taken around 1880. (Montgomery County. ADAH.)

# eleven
*Family Album*

Alabama writers reflect the agrarian traditions of the South, and the characters they create reveal the same strong sense of place, attachment to the land, to family, and to the homeplace as Alabamians have always shared. Pioneers moved into Alabama in family groups, and family members migrated to cities together or followed one another as soon as the first could find work and a place to live. Networks of kith and kin are woven through rural areas of the state to the inner city and to suburbia. For generations, grandparents remained on the farm or the homeplace, and grandchildren visited each summer.

Strong moral and religious values included within the family are basic to people's lives. They supply the security and the direction that allow confident independence and the full measure of personal growth. Life is often hard, and families are a bulwark against pain and grief. Extended families are a treasury of shared emotion, and children who grow up in strong, loving families have memories that help sustain them and shoulders to lean on in times of trouble.

Family albums do not include just the famous or the wealthy, the governor or the mayor, but also the memories of average Alabamians, sometimes the only record of a life well lived. Here then is a collection of Alabamians who constitute the strong threads in the fabric of society and a family album of Alabama.

This large family group from Selma posed for the photographer in their Sunday dress circa 1908. (Dallas County. ADAH.)

Below: The identification of this Pike County mother and son has been lost over time. The portrait was made circa 1915. (Pike County. Courtesy of the University of South Alabama Archives.)

The John Summers family of Opelika posed for this picture in the fall of 1895. Mr. Summers was seated on the left next to Lily Belle, cousin Gertie Dodson, Kate, and Marcia. Mrs. Summers sat on the bench with Carl, Ethel, and Ralph while Nelle stood in front. Reverend Gibson, a Methodist preacher, stood behind Mrs. Summers. The inclusion of the maid, Babe Carpenter, indicated her importance to the family at the same time her separation from the rest of the group represented the social distance between employers and domestic workers. An empty chair, like the one by which the maid stands, was often used to symbolize a missing or deceased loved one. (Lee County. Courtesy of Carl and Jesse Summers.)

Governor Thomas E. Kilby and his family were photographed at their home in Anniston circa 1920. Seated with Governor Kilby, far left, were Mrs. Kilby and Lewis J. Clark. Oscar Marchant Kilby, T. E. Kilby Jr., and Whitfield Clark Jr. stood behind them while Anne Kilby Porter sat beside baby Edith. (Calhoun County. Courtesy of Russell Collection, Public Library of Anniston and Calhoun County.)

John W. and Hattie Cook Gates of Helena posed for this informal portrait around 1920. Gates, a truck miner, was profiled as "Johnnie Fence" in *Up Before Daylight: Life Histories from the Alabama Writers' Project, 1938–1939*. Woodrow Hand describes Johnnie Fence this way: "[his] face bears the unmistakable mark of years underground. It is pockmarked and lined with blue scars—wounds that healed over coal dust. His hands are gnarled, with stubby fingers. Over all are the identifying blue marks." Johnnie and Hattie lived in an unpainted, slightly weather-worn bungalow of four or five rooms that they had owned for twenty years. Flowers dotted the front yard. A vegetable garden was on the side, and a chicken yard and a half-acre of corn were in the rear. Johnnie and Hattie had two children, a four-year-old girl and a twenty-year-old boy. Johnnie sent his son to Howard College for one year and arranged for him to work his way through the final three years. He also was able to send his daughter to college. Johnnie realized the importance of an education, having lost out on a job to a man who knew "triggermomity" and did better on the examination even though he was less experienced. Truck mining sprang up after the Alabama mining strike of 1920 and the national strike of 1922. After the big mines closed, entrepreneurs devised simple ways to bring coal out of the mines, a couple of cars at a time. Usually the truck mines did not last long because the available coal was taken out or the operators went broke. Paramount, the company Johnnie worked for, was better financed and more modern; however, the work was still sporadic. As Johnnie said: "Sometimes I go a week without hittin' a lick; then get called for Sunday, right when me'n Joan are all triggered up to go down to the Baptist church to Sunday school." As Hand noted, not all of the truck miners were "so fortunate as Johnnie Fence, who manages to keep a fairly even keel. He owns his own home and is content." (Shelby County. Courtesy of Debbie Pendleton.)

*181*

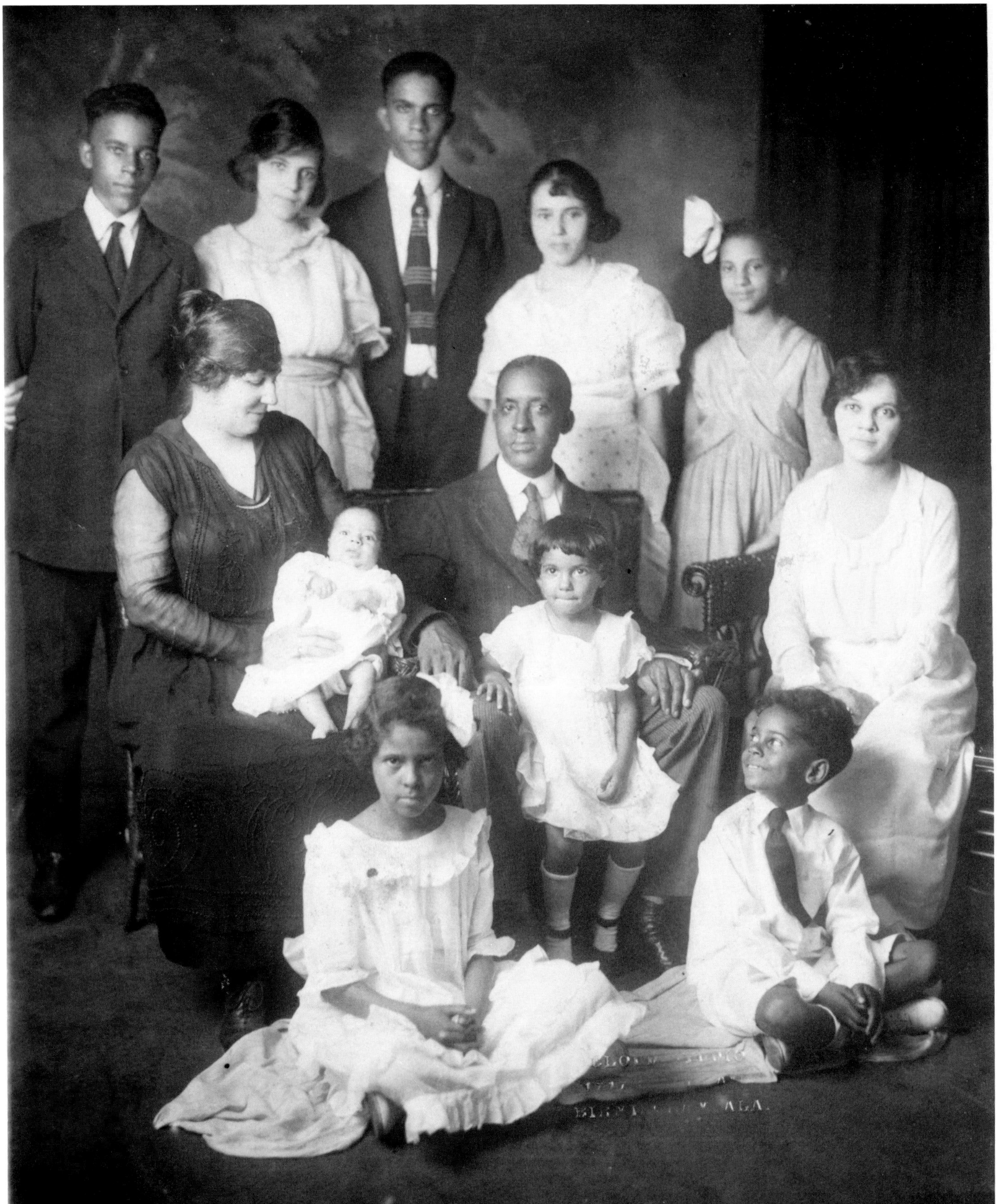

During World War II, General Courtney H. Hodges succeeded General Omar Bradley as commander of the First Army in August 1944. He led it through France, Belgium, Germany, and to the Czechoslovakian frontier by the war's end. General Hodges was greeted by his mother when he returned home after the war. (ADAH.)

Left: In October 1920, the Charles Morgan Harris family gathered in the Birmingham studio of photographer Hampton Cloud located on Seventeenth Street between Fourth and Fifth Avenues, North. Charles M. Harris and his sister, Hattie Hale Davenport, founded the Davenport and Harris Funeral Home in Birmingham in September 1899. Protective Industrial Insurance Company (PIICO) was an outgrowth of that business which is, today, the parent company of its progenitor. Both companies are still owned by the Harris family. In this portrait, Charles Harris, with daughter Sadye Harris James in his lap, sat next to his wife, Mattie, who held their first grandchild, Ira Emmett Evans Jr. Mr. and Mrs. Harris were surrounded by their other children (clockwise from top left): Walter Wellington Harris, Esq.; Blanche Harris Baugh Hardin; Charles Morgan Harris Jr., M.D.; Bernice Harris Sterling; Madeline Harris Davis; Clara Harris Evans, mother of the baby; Virgil Leon Harris; and Otis Harris Cole. (Jefferson County. Courtesy of the Birmingham Public Library Department of Archives and Manuscripts.)

This woman enjoyed a rest after a day of picking cotton. (ADAH.)

The Thompson homestead in Tuskegee was home to a wealthy Macon County family and frequently the scene of social and political events. The arch was constructed for President William McKinley's visit to Tuskegee Institute in 1898. On that trip, the president stopped at the Thompson's for lunch. This family portrait was taken in 1902. In the late twentieth century, the house was moved to Montgomery and renovated. In 1991, it opened as the Montgomery Visitor Center. (Macon County. ADAH.)

Below: The T. L. Thorson family of Thorsby, founded by a group of Scandinavians in the 1890s, enjoyed a prosperous farm life in Chilton County. The founders of the town included farmlands within its boundaries to provide a broad tax base for the school system. Thorsby became a thriving community of substantial homes such as this one. Family portraits, like this one taken on June 12, 1900, often gave individuals an opportunity to display what was most important to them, such as the son on the second-floor porch holding his horn and the daughter reading a book. (Chilton County. ADAH.)

This home in Escambia County was typical of those served by the Works Progress Administration (WPA) Housekeeping Aide program in the 1930s. (Escambia County. ADAH.)

This rare photograph of an unidentified young African-American girl is a tintype in a daguerreotype case. (ADAH.)

Hazel Copeland Burke of Fountain Heights in Birmingham posed for the family album in 1898. (Jefferson County. Courtesy of Leah Rawls Atkins.)

Tallulah Bankhead, pictured here circa 1915 at age fourteen, became an acclaimed stage and film actress in the United States and England. She came from a family as renowned in politics as she was in the theater: her father was William Brockman Bankhead, Speaker of the House during the Roosevelt administration; her uncle was John H. Bankhead II, a senator; and her grandfather was John Hollis Bankhead, also a senator. (Montgomery County. ADAH.)

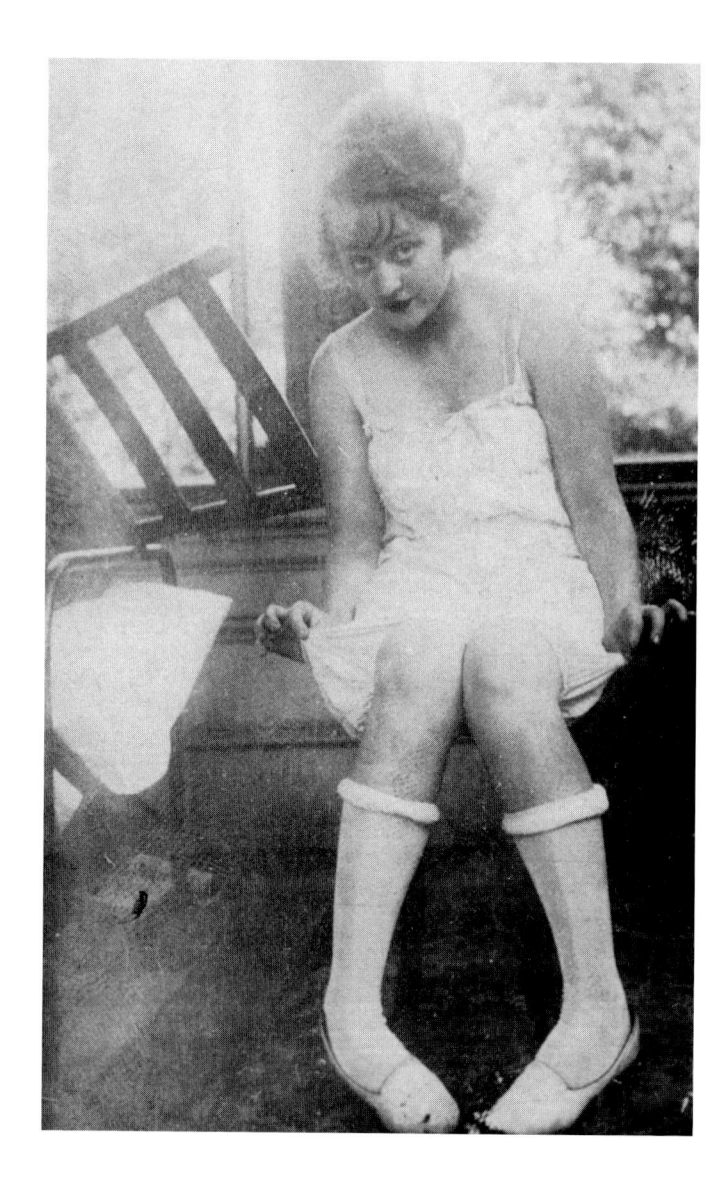

Emma Sansom became a heroine of the Confederacy in 1863 when she was only fifteen years old. By leading General Nathan Bedford Forrest's soldiers across a shallow part of Black Creek near Gadsden so they could continue their pursuit of Union General Abel Streight and his men, she secured her place in Alabama history. In November 1863, the Alabama legislature adopted a series of joint resolutions awarding Sansom a section of land and a gold medal. Some of the land was surveyed and sold for Confederate scrip. Sansom married C. B. Johnson of the Tenth Alabama Infantry in 1864, and, in 1896, they moved to Texas. This photograph is from the original portrait by Samuel Hoffman presented in 1902 by the Alabama Division, United Daughters of the Confederacy to the Alabama Department of Archives and History. (ADAH.)

Ruby Parsons Monfee, the oldest daughter of a Prattville farmer, was photographed snapping beans in the 1930s. Many of the photographs taken by WPA (Works Progress Administration) photographers deliberately attempted to show the negative side of rural life in Alabama during the Depression. This photograph gives proof to the old saying that money can't buy happiness. Mrs. Monfee is happy, well dressed, and productive. (Autauga County. ADAH.)

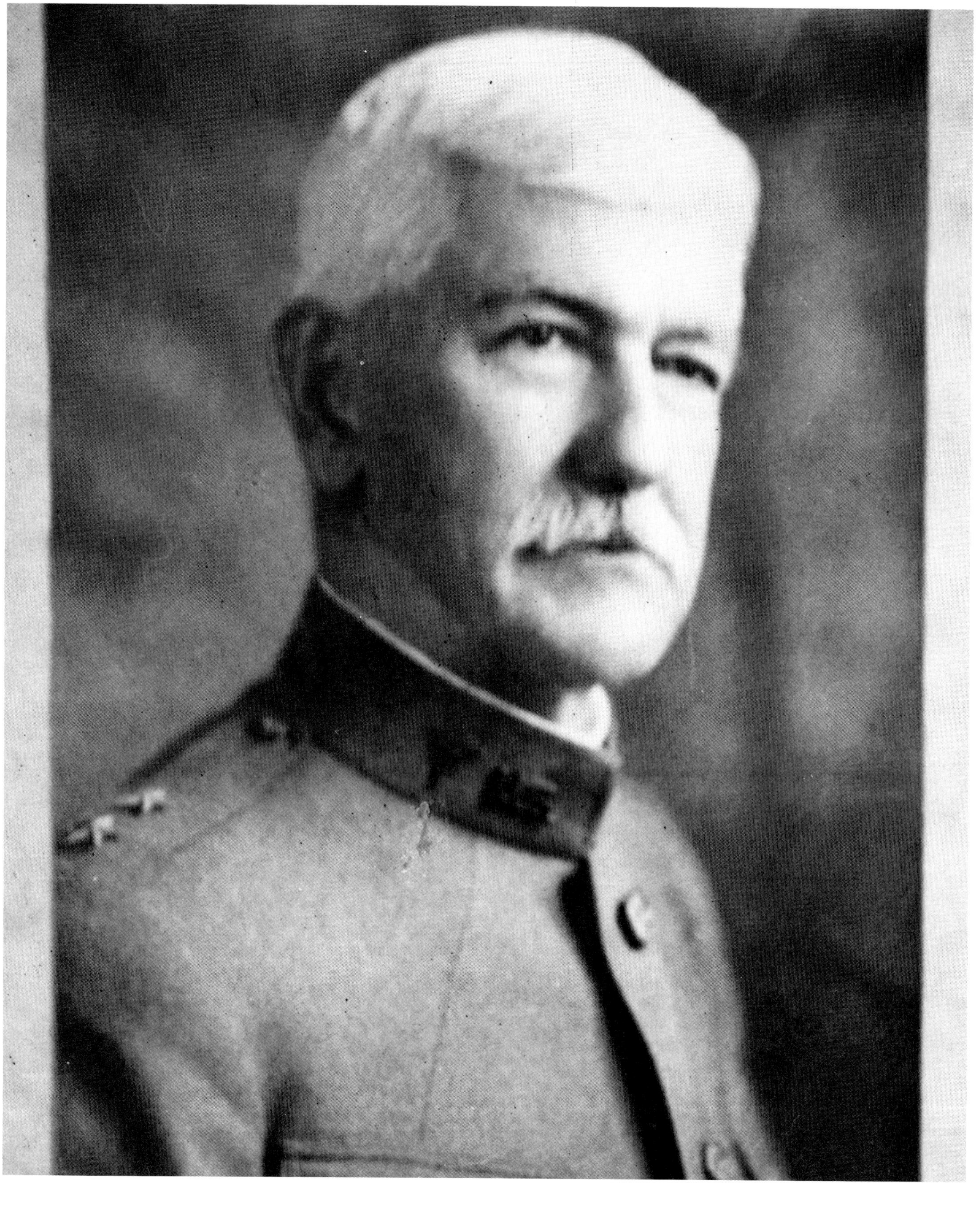

Arthur McKimmon Brown was the first Negro surgeon in the U.S. Army. Dr. Brown was appointed by President McKinley to the post of assistant surgeon in the Spanish-American War with the rank of first lieutenant in the U.S. Tenth Cavalry stationed at Santiago, Cuba. A graduate of the University of Michigan and Lincoln University near Philadelphia, Dr. Brown practiced medicine and surgery in Birmingham for over fifty years and was president of the Association of Colored Physicians and Surgeons in the United States, Cuba, Puerto Rico, and the Philippines. (Jefferson County. ADAH.)

Julia Tutwiler was one of eleven children of Henry Tutwiler who ran Greene Springs Academy, one of Alabama's most outstanding private schools before the Civil War. Educated at her father's school, she developed a strong commitment to better education for all Alabamians. Tutwiler, who taught at Tuscaloosa Female College for several years, believed the first step was to train more and better teachers. In 1881, Tutwiler became coprincipal and teacher at Livingston Female Academy, and, in 1890, she became sole principal of the school which by then was known as Alabama Normal College and provided teacher training for women. She remained in that position for the next twenty years. In 1892, she persuaded the University of Alabama to allow women to enroll, and she was partly responsible for the establishment of an industrial school for girls at Montevallo. Tutwiler also was active in prison reform, actively and effectively lobbying for improved living conditions for prisoners, a separate prison for women, and educational programs for inmates. (Sumter County. ADAH.)

Left: Dr. William Crawford Gorgas, a doctor from Tuscaloosa and surgeon general of the U.S. Army, was given the task of stopping the yellow fever epidemic which caused a large number of casualties among workers building the Panama Canal in the early 1900s. Although the popular theory at that time was that the disease was transmitted by rats, Dr. Walter Reed was able to prove that it was spread by mosquitoes and could be controlled by chemicals. Gorgas became a national hero for cleaning up the Canal Zone (Tuscaloosa County. ADAH.)

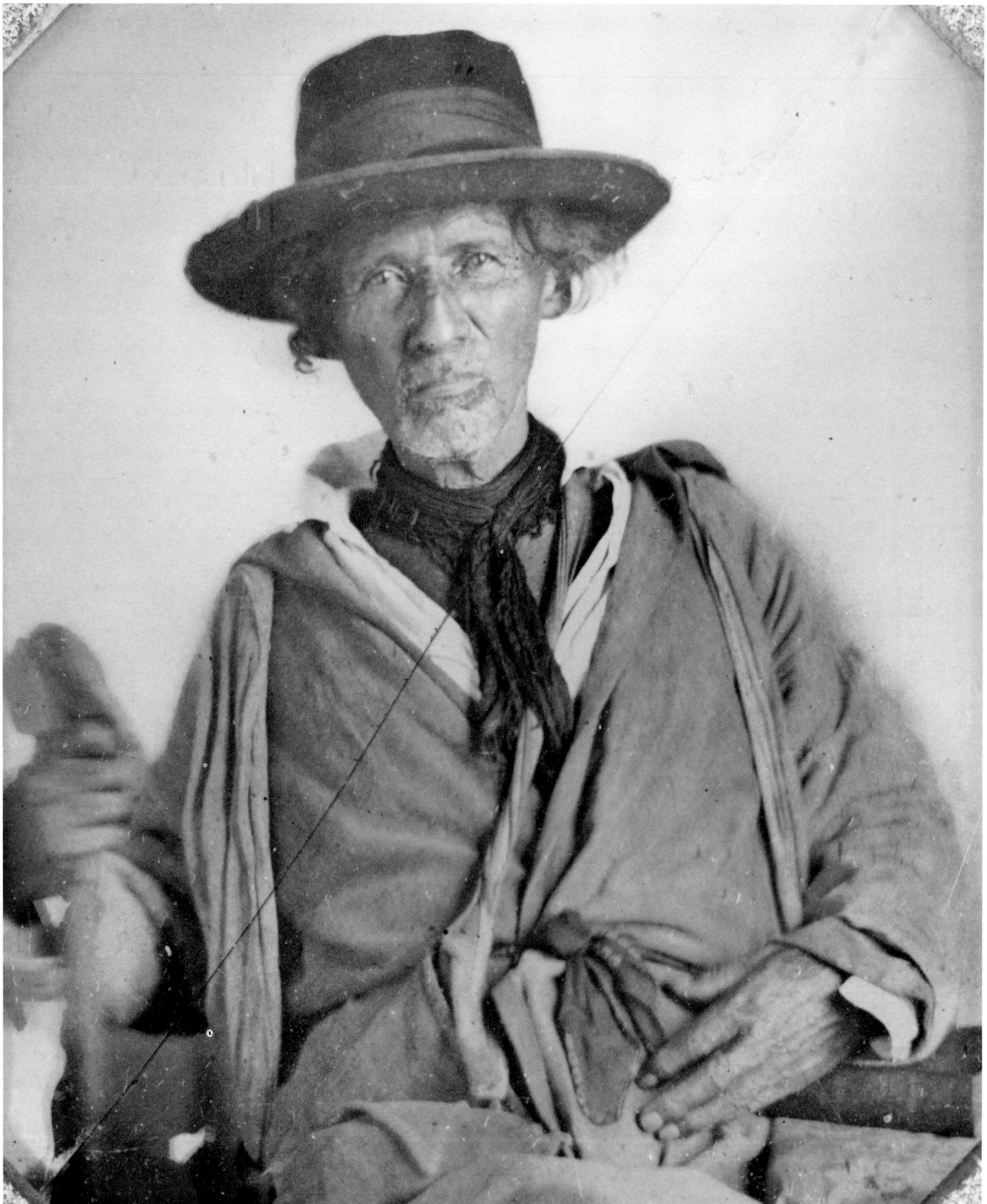

Reverend James Perry of Eufaula posed in the mid-1930s for a photographer for the Alabama Writers' Project. The Alabama Writers' Project collection provides significant documentation of black and white Alabamians and of their lives, from their homes and domestic activities to their work and recreation. (Barbour County. ADAH.)

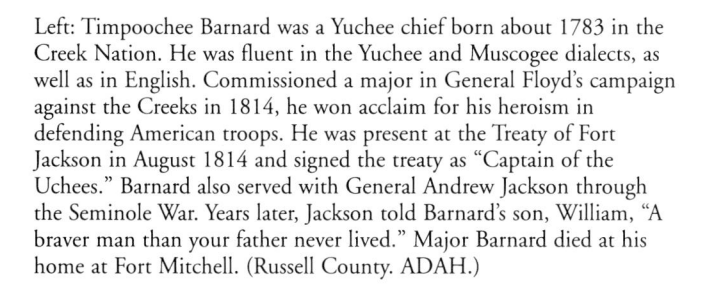

At a 1912 reunion in Macon, Georgia, Mrs. Townes Randolph Leigh of Montgomery, matron for the Army of Tennessee, posed with the four brigade commanders of the Alabama Division of the United Confederate Veterans—General Weathers of Roanoke, General John B. Fuller of Montgomery, General G. R. Thompson of Tuscumbia, and General H. Austill of Mobile. (Macon, Ga. ADAH.)

Mary Lee Simpson was the daughter of R. O. Simpson, a founder of the Snow Hill Institute for black students. She was a teacher at the Alabama Girls' Industrial School, which later became the University of Montevallo, where she also gave speech recitals and painted. At the time of her death in 1948, she was chairman of the Board of Trustees at Snow Hill. Simpson took a series of photographs documenting African-Americans in Alabama around the turn of the century. Her beautifully hand-tinted photographs captured everyday activities of rural Alabamians around 1900. This picture of a young white woman and an older African-American woman, who might have been the nurse who helped raise her, is from the Simpson collection. The pose suggests an intimacy and mutual reliance between the two. (Wilcox County. ADAH.)

Left: Timpoochee Barnard was a Yuchee chief born about 1783 in the Creek Nation. He was fluent in the Yuchee and Muscogee dialects, as well as in English. Commissioned a major in General Floyd's campaign against the Creeks in 1814, he won acclaim for his heroism in defending American troops. He was present at the Treaty of Fort Jackson in August 1814 and signed the treaty as "Captain of the Uchees." Barnard also served with General Andrew Jackson through the Seminole War. Years later, Jackson told Barnard's son, William, "A braver man than your father never lived." Major Barnard died at his home at Fort Mitchell. (Russell County. ADAH.)

This group posed in front of the office of the Dothan Populist newspaper, the *Wire-grass Siftings*, before an outing. The sow and her piglets outside the front door also seemed to enjoy the day. (Houston County. Courtesy of the Houston Love Memorial Library.)

Mary Lee Simpson captured for posterity this group of four young children perched on a fence in Furman in rural Wilcox County. (Wilcox County. ADAH.)

These two farm women from Eden came to town to shop, probably on a Saturday afternoon, in the 1930s. This Farm Security Administration (FSA) photograph was taken by Dorothea Lange, one of the well-known photographers who participated in FSA and Works Progress Administration projects. (St. Clair County. Courtesy of the Library of Congress.)

This group of young women posed in a Macon County peach orchard around 1930. The photograph taken by the Alabama Cooperative Extension Service at Auburn is entitled "Two kinds of Macon County peaches." (Macon County. ADAH.)

The Albert Weeks family of Fairhope posed circa 1920 for a family photograph outside the studio of Stewart, The Picture Man. Mr. Weeks delivered ice in the community. (Baldwin County. Courtesy of Flora Maye Simmons.)

Apache Indians, who had been held at forts in Pensacola and St. Augustine, Florida, since 1886, were reunited at Mt. Vernon in 1888. There they were allowed to construct homes, tend gardens, and attend church and school. Many of the young were sent away to school at Carlisle, Pennsylvania, and a number of the men enlisted in the U.S. Army. The Apaches were transferred to Ft. Sill, Oklahoma, in 1894, where they remained as prisoners of war until 1913. Apaches from several bands were held at Mt. Vernon. Among them were Geronimo and members of his "group of hostiles" which had surrendered in 1886. They are from left to right: Chihuahua, Naiche—the son of Cochise, Loco, Nana, and Geronimo. These Apache leaders were photographed by Silas Orlando Trippe, a jeweler and amateur photographer from Selma hired by the War Department. (Mobile County. ADAH.)

Students posed in front of Miss Mary Avery's School in Greensboro in 1884. Miss Avery is seventh from the left standing on the porch in a checked dress with a dark bow. (Hale County. ADAH.)

This farmhouse was typical of many rural Alabama homes in 1939. During spring cleaning, the wife and mother in this home sunned her hand-made quilts and bed clothes to keep them fresh. This photograph was taken as part of the work of the Alabama Writers' Project. (Coffee County. Courtesy of the Library of Congress.)

Winnie McIntosh of Kennedy followed the generations old tradition of hand scrubbing, rinsing, and boiling clothes until they were clean. The large straw hat and the shade of the peach tree perhaps provided some respite from the heat. This domestic scene, recorded in the late 1930s, was repeated daily at homes across Alabama. (Lamar County. Courtesy of Mary Davis Elmore.)

Mary Lee Simpson recorded this woman sweeping her yard with a twig broom. Swept yards were a tradition in black and white families in Alabama, especially in South Alabama, for much of the nineteenth and early twentieth centuries. (Wilcox County. ADAH.)

Right: As Alabamians, we have inherited a rich legacy shaped over ten thousand years by the people who have lived on the land now known as Alabama. That legacy provides the foundation on which we will build the future and offers the tools with which to shape the twenty-first century. Our legacy is given to us in trust, and it is the responsibility of each of us to nurture it and pass it on to future generations. Carley Suther of Anniston tends her legacy as she waters plants on the grave of her great-great-great-grandfather, Sergeant Richard A. Jones, who lived in Elyton and served in Company G of the Forty-third Alabama Infantry. He surrendered with the Forty-third at Appomattox Courthouse at the end of the Civil War. Jones and his wife, Jennie Elizabeth, are buried in Birmingham's Oak Hill Cemetery. (Jefferson County. Courtesy of the *Birmingham News*.)

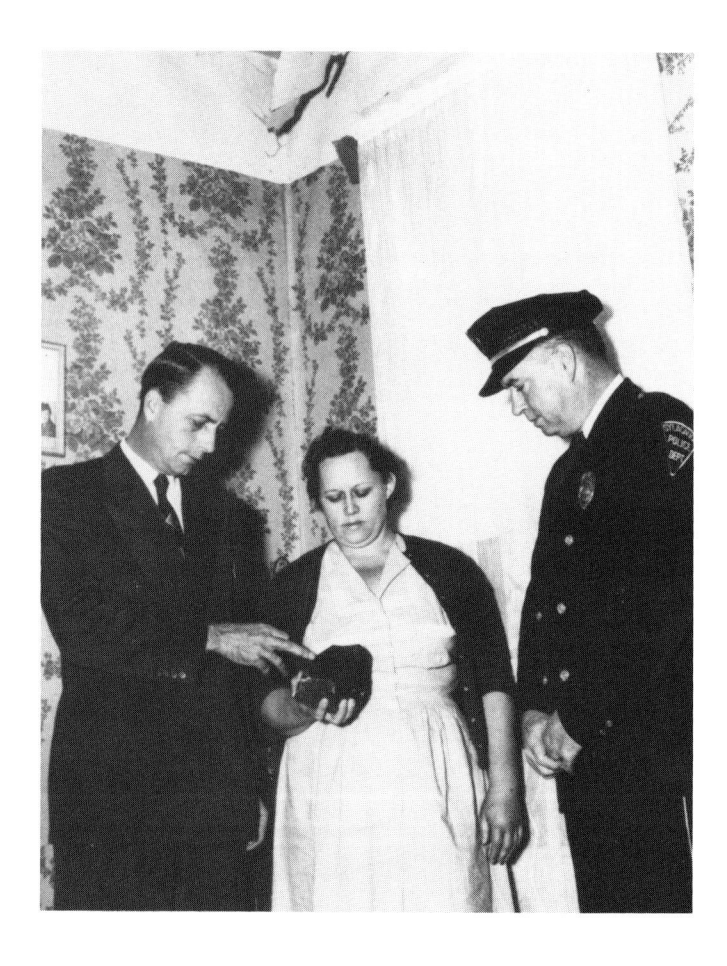

One hundred and twenty-one years after stars fell on Alabama in a spectacular meteor shower, one Alabama woman had a different experience with a falling star. In 1954, Ann Hodges was lying on the sofa in her home in Sylacauga when an eight and a half pound meteorite, traveling at 270 miles per hour, crashed through the roof, careened off two walls and a radio console, and struck her on the wrist, arm, thigh, and abdomen. Hodges' experience is the only recorded instance of a person being struck by a meteorite. (Talladega County. Courtesy of the Alabama Museum of Natural History, University of Alabama Museums.)

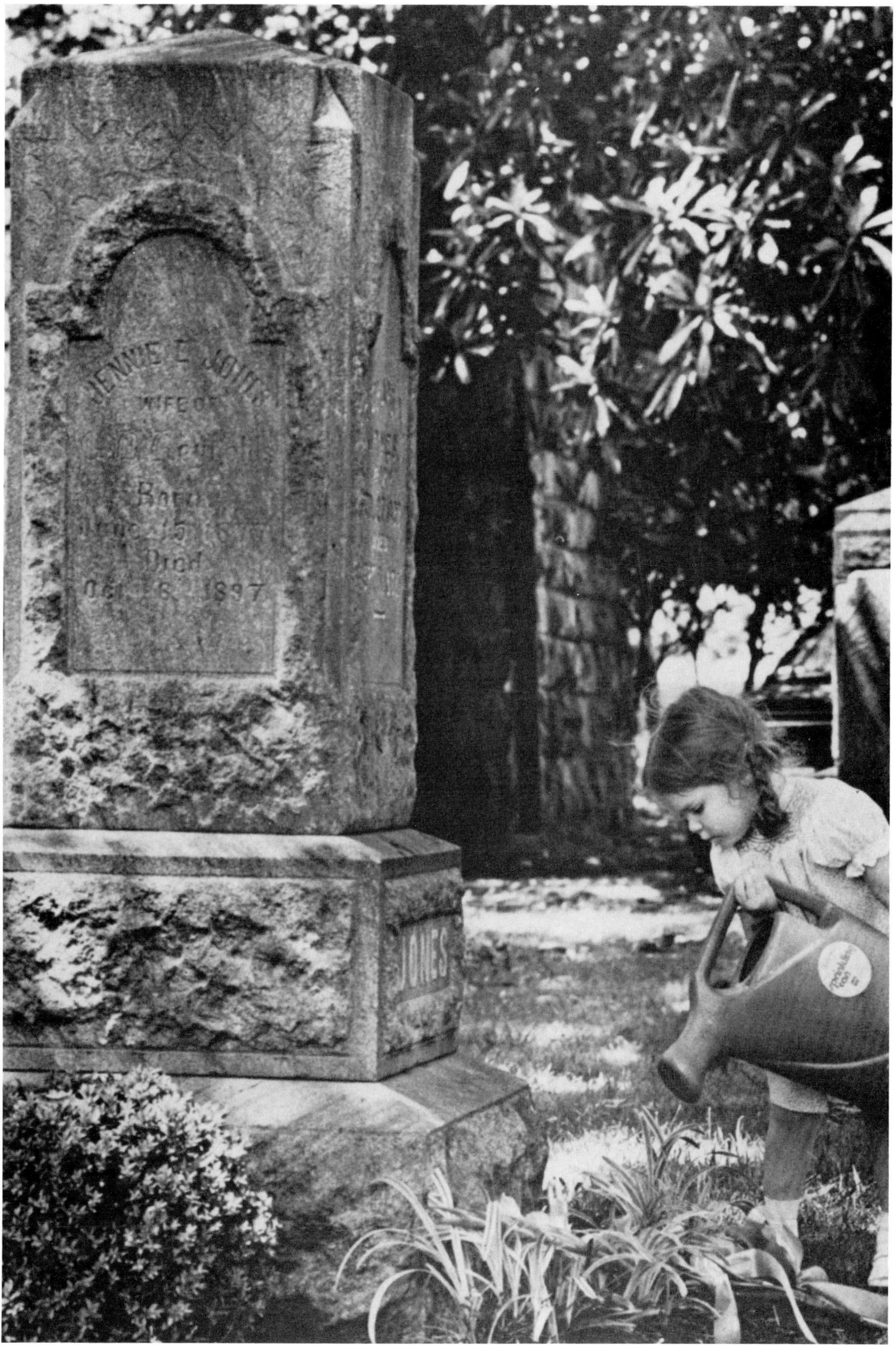
WIFE OF
JONES

# twelve
*Conclusion*

The future may seem to be a thing of shadowy portents, whispered hints, and vague illumination—impossible to photograph and amenable to description only through the art of prophecy and divination. But the future is not a foreign land divorced from everything we know and understand. It is not a realm where only flights of fancy and imagination live. Time is a seamless line: it is only our perspective and point of view that gives meaning to the tenses of past, present, and future.

A knowledge of their past can help Alabamians—the men and women of today—face the challenges of the twenty-first century. The state has vast water and natural resources that remain untapped. Huntsville's Development Board boasts an enviable record for convincing industry to locate in the region near the Marshall Space Flight Center. Mobile has a modern convention center on the Bay, which is bringing new visitors to the area. Birmingham has moved from being the top blue-collar worker, mine and mill, heavy-industry district to assuming leadership in medical technology, service industries, and publication fields. Montgomery is experiencing a construction and cultural boom. Dothan is growing rapidly in the Wiregrass. Anniston, Gadsden, Florence, Decatur, Auburn, Tuscaloosa, and Opelika are enjoying prosperity.

The state's historical attractions—antebellum homes in the Tennessee Valley, at Eufaula, and across the Black Belt; the Space and Rocket Center and Alabama's Constitution Village in Huntsville; the Department of Archives and History, Old Alabama Town, and the restored 1851 Capitol at Montgomery; Civil War and civil rights sites at Birmingham, Montgomery, and Selma; and dozens of historical districts increase tourism each year. The warm climate and white Gulf beaches attract winter and summer tourists to the areas around Dauphin Island, Fort Morgan, Gulf Shores, and Orange Beach.

Public libraries that feature programs for both children and adults, local art associations and writers' support groups, city festivals, pop concerts, fine art and natural history museums, science centers, and the Alabama Shakespeare Festival enrich the cultural life of the state. Good fishing lakes and a series of nationally recognized golf courses provide numerous places for leisure.

The promise of Alabama's future is all around us. It grows out of the bravery of the past, the determination to succeed in the face of sharp adversity, and the fundamental values without which human society becomes a fearful place of conflict and dissension. We see the future as we drive our highways and follow the ribbons of our magnificent rivers. The future surrounds us with the busy activity at the State Docks at Mobile and

The beef cattle industry is big business in Alabama, representing a $3 billion return to the state's economy. The thirty thousand producers receive annually nearly $400 million in cash receipts from the sale of cattle and calves, placing the cattle industry second among all farm commodities in Alabama. These producers, located in every county in the state, own 1.8 million head of beef cattle. The state's cattle producers are recognized for the outstanding quality of their cattle, as well as top management practices of their land and the environment. Today's cattle producer cares for his land and livestock and works to preserve the heritage of his family farm in order to pass it on to future generations. (Courtesy of the Alabama Cattlemen's Association.)

the concentration of engineering talents sired by the space industries of Huntsville. The future is in the streets of Birmingham, an ever-growing commercial headquarters for the complex world of business.

We are looking at the future when we explore the impact and potential of the Mercedes-Benz investments in our state—and the other investments that will come. The future is already with us in our schools and universities. They are at work today in hopes of tomorrow with a stream of future generations flowing through their grades and reminding us that life is process.

Problems, troubles, and difficulties are the basic ingredients of human society. They are obstacles when we refuse to solve them. They are steps of progress and advancement when we deal with them, and the solutions to problems are the mileposts toward a better future. Alabama's history of struggles and of accomplishments over adversity has been a time of preparation. It has brought us to where we are today and provided us the tools for shaping our future. History is a forge, tempering our metal for a stronger future.

The legacy of Alabama's history is not a burden to be carried, not a heavy load forgotten or a treasure to be stored away for private viewing. Alabama's legacy—preserved in the records, manuscripts, photographs, and artifacts of our past—is a priceless gift to every citizen, a book of instruction, and a manual of social wisdom.

Alabama's history provides our marching orders for the future.

# bibliography

Abernethy, Thomas Perkins. *The Formative Period in Alabama, 1815–1828*. University: University of Alabama Press, 1965.

Armes, Ethel. *The Story of Coal and Iron in Alabama*. 1910. Reprint. Birmingham: Bookkeepers Press, 1972.

Atkins, Leah Rawls. *The Valley and the Hills: An Illustrated History of Birmingham and Jefferson County*. Woodland Hills, Calif.: Windsor Publication, 1981.

Barnard, William D. *Dixiecrats and Democrats: Alabama Politics, 1942–1950*. University: University of Alabama Press, 1974.

Barney, William L. *The Secessionist Impulse: Alabama and Mississippi in 1860*. Princeton, N. J.: University Press, 1974.

Bond, Horace Mann. *Negro Education in Alabama: A Study in Cotton and Steel*. Washington, D. C.: Associated Publishers, 1939.

Boyd, Minnie Clare. *Alabama in the Fifties: A Social Study*. New York: Columbia University Press, 1931.

Brantley, William H. *Banking in Alabama, 1816–1860*. 2 vols. Birmingham: Birmingham Printing Co., 1961.

Braund, Kathryn E. Holland. *Deerskins and Duffels: The Creek Indian Trade with Anglo-America, 1685–1815*. Lincoln: University of Nebraska Press, 1993.

Carmer, Carl. *Stars Fell on Alabama*. New York: Farrar and Rinehart, 1934.

Clark, E. Culpepper. *The Schoolhouse Door: Segregation's Last Stand at the University of Alabama*. New York: Oxford University Press, 1993.

Doster, James F. *Railroad in Alabama Politics, 1875–1914*. University: University of Alabama Press, 1957.

Fleming, Walter L. *Civil War and Reconstruction in Alabama*. 1905. Reprint. Gloucester, Mass.: Peter Smith, 1949.

Flynt, J. Wayne. *Poor But Proud: Alabama's Poor Whites*. Tuscaloosa: University of Alabama Press, 1989.

Going, Allen J. *Bourbon Democracy in Alabama, 1874–1890*. 1951. Reprint. Tuscaloosa: University of Alabama Press, 1992.

Grafton, Carl, and Anne Permaloff. *Big Mules and Branchheads: James E. Folsom and Political Power in Alabama*. Athens: University of Georgia Press, 1985.

Hamilton, Peter J. *Colonial Mobile*. 1897. 1910. Reprint. Edited with introduction and annotations by Charles G. Summersell. University: University of Alabama Press, 1976.

Hamilton, Virginia Van der Veer. *Hugo Black: The Alabama Years*. Baton Rouge: Louisiana University Press, 1972.

Harlan, Louis R. *Booker T. Washington: The Making of a Black Leader*. New York: Oxford University Press, 1972.

Kelley, Robin D. *Hammer and Hoe: Alabama Communists During the Great Depression*. Chapel Hill: University of North Carolina Press, 1990.

Kolchin, Peter. *First Freedom: The Response of Alabama Blacks to Emancipation and Reconstruction*. Westport, Conn.: Greenwood Press, 1972.

Lesher, Stephen. *George Wallace: American Populist*. Reading, Mass.: Addison-Wesley, 1993.

Mobile's striking new Convention Center on the banks of the Mobile River was dedicated in 1993. (Mobile County. Photograph by Dan Brothers. Courtesy of the Alabama Bureau of Tourism and Travel.)

McMillan, Malcolm Cook. *Constitutional Development in Alabama, 1798–1901: A Study in Politics, the Negro, and Sectionalism*. 1955. Reprint. Spartanburg, S.C.: Reprint Co., 1978.

———. *The Disintegration of a Confederate State: Three Governors and Alabama's Wartime Home Front, 1861–1865*. Macon: Mercer University Press, 1986.

Mayfield, Sara. *Exiles from Paradise: Zelda and Scott Fitzgerald*. New York: Delacorte Press, 1971.

Norrell, Robert J. *Reaping the Whirlwind: The Civil Rights Movement in Tuskegee*. New York: Alfred A. Knopf, 1985.

Owen, Thomas M. *History of Alabama and Dictionary of Alabama Biography*. 4 vols. Chicago: S. J. Clarke, 1921.

Owsley, Frank L., Jr. *Struggle for the Gulf Borderlands: The Creek War and the Battle of New Orleans, 1812–1815*. Gainesville: University Presses of Florida, 1981.

Rogers, William Warren. *The One-Gallused Rebellion: Agrarianism in Alabama, 1865–1896*. Baton Rouge: Louisiana State University Press, 1970.

Rogers, William Warren, Robert David Ward, Leah Rawls Atkins, and Wayne Flynt. *Alabama: The History of a Deep South State*. Tuscaloosa: University of Alabama Press, 1994.

Salmond, John A. *The Conscience of a Lawyer: Clifford J. Durr and American Civil Liberties, 1899–1975*. Tuscaloosa: University of Alabama Press, 1990.

Southerland, Henry DeLeon, Jr., and Jerry Elijah Brown. *The Federal Road through Georgia, the Creek Nation, and Alabama, 1806–1836*. Tuscaloosa: University of Alabama Press, 1989.

Thomas, Mary Martha. *The New Women in Alabama: Social Reform and Suffrage 1890–1920*. Tuscaloosa: University of Alabama Press, 1992.

Thornton, J. Mills, III. *Politics and Power in a Slave Society: Alabama, 1800–1860*. Baton Rouge: Louisiana State University Press, 1978.

Although the official grand opening was on June 1, 1985, the Tennessee-Tombigbee Waterway opened for commercial traffic on January 14–16, 1985, when the first tow traveled the length of the waterway. That tow was the completion of a dream that had begun more than one hundred years earlier when the first survey on an alternate route to the Gulf of Mexico was conducted in 1874. The Tenn–Tom Waterway forms a 234 mile long, 300 feet wide by 9 feet deep transportation artery connecting west-central Alabama and northeastern Mississippi. Made up of a series of ten locks, it connects that part of the nation with the existing 16,000-mile inland waterway system and shortens shipping distances for many inland ports by over 800 miles. In 1994, over 7,905,000 tons of commodities—forest products such as timber and wood chips, petroleum by-products, crushed rock, and grains—were shipped by barge via the Tenn-Tom. Public and private interests have invested more than $86 million to develop ports, terminals, and waterfront industrial parks along the waterway. In addition, over 13,000 acres of land were set aside for development of recreation areas for camping, picnicking, hunting, fishing, hiking, biking, and boating. The waterway also features visitor and environmental education centers along its length. This barge moved through Lock C at Fulton, Mississippi, across the state line from Marion County. (Courtesy U.S. Army Corps of Engineers.)

Ward, Robert David, and William Warren Rogers. *Labor Revolt in Alabama: The Great Strike of 1894*. University: University of Alabama Press, 1965.

Wiggins, Sarah Woolfork. *The Scalawag in Alabama Politics, 1865–1881*. University: University of Alabama Press, 1977.

Williams, Benjamin Buford. *A Literary History of Alabama: The Nineteenth Century*. Rutherford, N.J.: Fairleigh Dickinson University Press, 1979.

Williams, Roger M. *Sing a Sad Song: The Life of Hank Williams*. New York: Ballentine Books, 1970.

Yarbrough, Tinsley E. *Judge Johnson and Human Rights in Alabama*. University: University of Alabama Press, 1981.

# index

**A**
Alabama, C.S.S., 39
Alabama A & M University, 58, 167
Alabama Anthropological Society, 14
Alabama Cooperative Extension Service, 62, 63, 193
Alabama Department of Archives and History, 6, 7, 14, 28, 39, 90, 187
Alabama Dry Dock and Shipbuilding Company, 50, 94
Alabama Equal Suffrage Association, 27
Alabama National Guard, 39, 47, 127
Alabama Power Company, 9, 91, 92
Alabama River, 9, 18, 19, 35, 69, 73, 97, 149
Alabama State University, 142, 167
Aliceville, 50, 117
Alexander City, 7, 88, 194
Anniston, 74, 87, 113, 136, 155, 181, 196, 198
Athens, 121
Auburn, 59, 66, 110, 120, 193, 198, 207
Auburn University (East Alabama Male College; Alabama Agricultural and Mechanical College; Alabama Polytechnic Institute), 58, 59, 62, 110, 120, 136, 143, 144, 164, 169
Auburn University at Montgomery, 144
Autauga County, 58, 87, 122, 187
Avondale Mills Corporation, 88, 94

**B**
Baggett, Agnes, 35
Baldwin County, 8, 16, 38, 91, 139, 172, 193, 206
Bankhead, Senator John H., II, 29, 186
Bankhead, Tallulah, 186
Barbour County, 31, 33, 57, 136, 150, 153, 191
Barnard, Timpoochee, 191
Battle of Holy Ground, 16
Battle of Horseshoe Bend, 7, 16, 17, 70, 99
Battle of Mobile Bay, 38, 42
Battle of Selma, 41, 42
Bessemer, 114
Bibb County, 9, 82
Bibb, Governor William Wyatt, 18, 19

Birmingham, 27, 31, 34, 41, 46, 71, 74, 76, 78, 80, 85, 87, 88, 113,116, 119, 123, 125, 130, 138, 142, 144, 152, 155, 165, 166, 169, 170, 176, 183, 186, 189, 196, 198, 199, 204, 205, 207
Birmingham Black Barons, 165
Birmingham Civil Rights Institute, 204
Black Warrior River, 69, 71
Blount County, 5
Brannon, Peter A., 7, 14
Brewer, Governor Albert, 35
Brewton, 122
Brookley Field, 46, 50
Brown, Arthur McKimmon, 189
Bryant, Paul "Bear," 169
Bullock County, 30
Butler County, 66, 177, 207

**C**
Cahaba River, 9, 18, 19
Cahawba, 18, 19, 127
Calhoun County, 66, 74, 75, 87, 131, 133, 136, 142, 155, 181
Camden, 120
Camp McClellan (Fort McClellan), 45, 46, 155
Campbell, Thomas Monroe, 144
Carbon Hill, 84
Carver, Dr. George Washington, 60, 62, 144
Centreville, 9
Chambers County, 131
Chattahoochee River, 69
Cherokee County, 1
Chilton County, 92, 184, 206
Choctaw County, 135
Citronelle, 42
Clarke County, 38
Clay County, 132, 163
Cleburne County, 127
Cleveland, 5
Coffee County, 60, 62, 65, 195
Colbert County, 68, 93, 105
Coley, Judge C. J., 7
Comer, Governor B. B., 88
Conecuh County, 30, 44
Continental Gin Company, 87
Coosa County, 92, 130

Coosa River, 69, 158
Cottage Grove, 130
Covington County, 154, 170
Crenshaw County, 121, 146
Craig Field, 46, 78
Cullman, 76, 114, 123,
Cullman County, 76, 123, 150, 206

**D**
Dale County, 51, 62, 175
Dallas County, 18, 24, 35, 36, 57, 64, 126, 127, 180
Dauphin Island, 16, 198
Davis, Jefferson, 22, 37, 39,
Decatur, 52, 87, 114, 148, 177, 198
DeKalb County, 4, 13, 55, 119, 206
Demopolis, 22, 69, 70, 155
Dixon, Governor Frank, 31
Dothan, 87, 192, 198, 207

**E**
Edmund Pettus Bridge, 35
Eden, 192
Eighteenth Alabama Infantry, 102
Elmore County, 73, 91
Elyton, 196
Elyton Land Company, 88, 119
Ensley, 85
Enterprise, 60
Escambia County, 16, 150, 185,
Etowah County, 33, 55, 64, 139, 175
Eufaula, 31, 57, 69, 136, 153, 155, 191, 198
Eutaw, 100, 130
Evans, Walker, 176
Evergreen, 30, 44

**F**
Fairhope, 172, 193
Fairhope Single Tax Colony, 172
Fayette County, 30
Farragut, Admiral David G., 38
Florence, 51, 69, 71, 110, 142, 198
Folsom, Governor James E. "Big Jim," 31, 33
Folsom, Governor James E., Jr., 33, 169
Fort Lewis, 16
Fort Mims, 16
Fort Morgan, 38, 198
Fort Payne, 114, 119
Fort Rucker (Camp Rucker), 46, 51
Forty-third Alabama Infantry, 196
Fourth Aviation Squadron, 48
Franklin County, 62
Furman, 104, 192

**G**
Gadsden, 30, 33, 71, 113, 139, 187, 198, 207
Gee's Bend, 10, 135, 149, 156
Geneva County, 80
Georgiana, 177
Geronimo, 194
Gorgas, William Crawford, 189
Graves, Governor Bibb, 28, 29, 140
Graves, Dixie, 29
Greene County, 100, 130
Greensboro, 195
Greenville, 122, 207
Grove Oak, 4
Gulf Shores, 8, 198
Gunter Field, 46, 78
Guntersville, 69, 171

Right: Communications in Alabama has changed dramatically since 1879 when the first telephone system was installed in Mobile. The state has come a long way from the dirt roads of that era—all the way to today's Information Superhighway. With over 1.7 million access lines, BellSouth is the state's largest telecommunications company, serving 78 percent of Alabama's residences and businesses.

Today, Alabamians have access to the world's foremost information resources through advanced digital switching systems and over 100,000 miles of fiber optic cable, each one capable of carrying the equivalent of 30,000 phone calls simultaneously—voice, video, or data. Advanced technology and local connnections to a worldwide telecommunications network enables each Alabamian to live, learn, and do business more quickly and more efficiently than ever before.

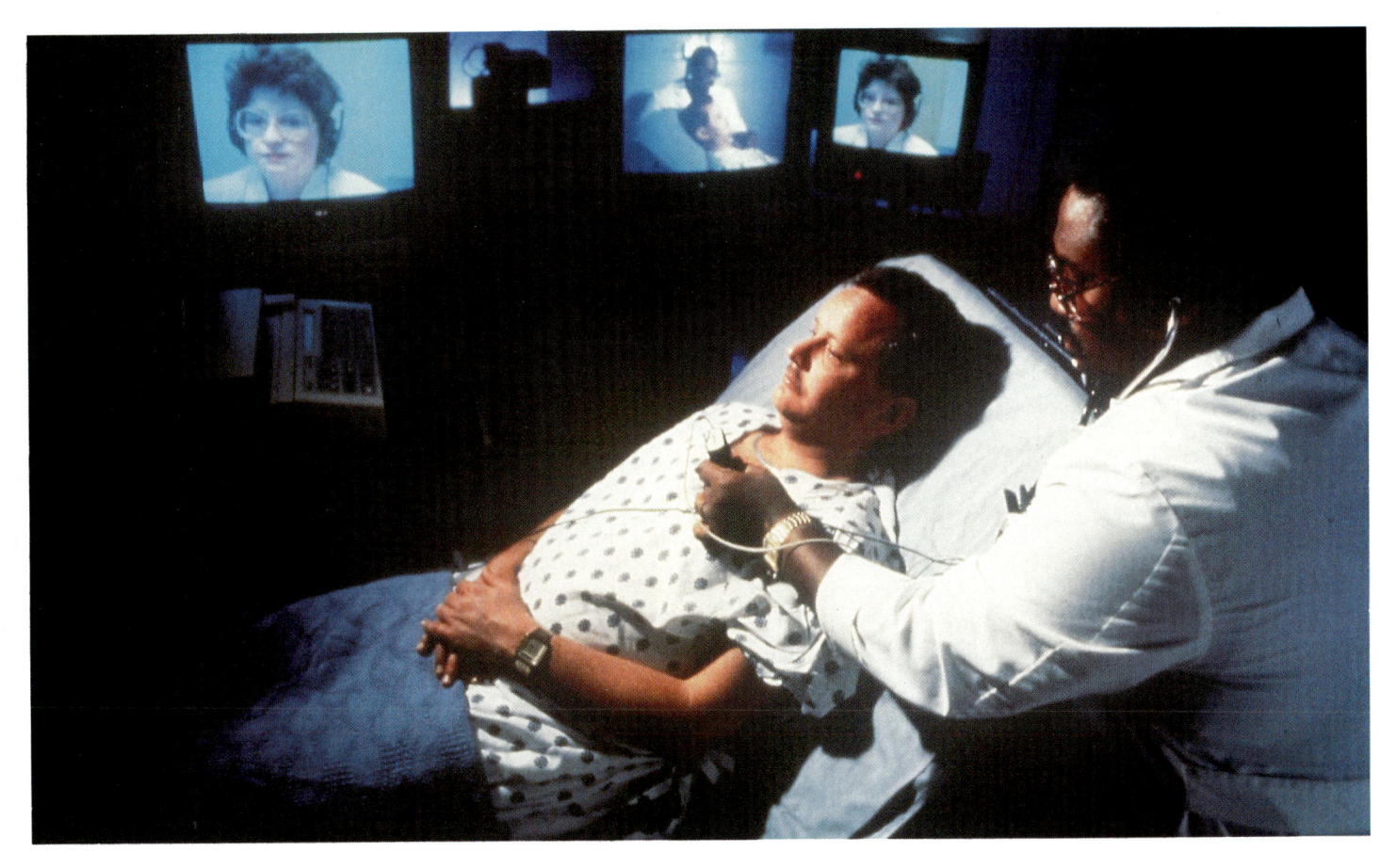

Leading-edge telecommunications networks can make world class health care easily accessible in every community, benefiting every person. This interactive video system brings the specialists to the patient. (Photograph by Alen Mac Weene, Copyright 1991. Courtesy of BellSouth.)

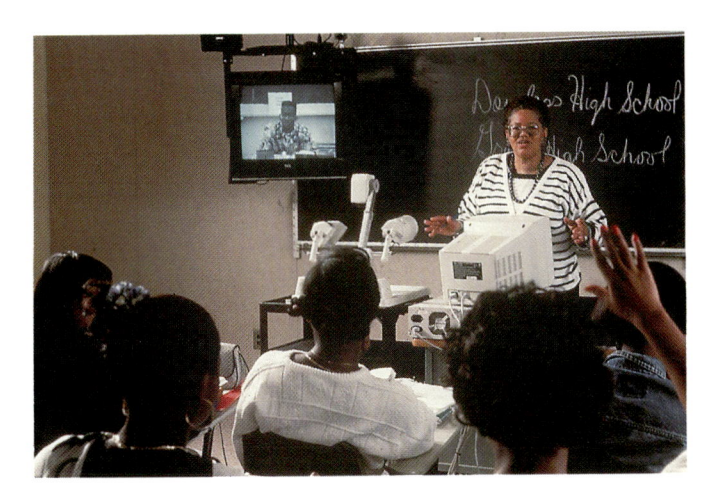

Learning was once defined by what was between the two corners of a book or within the four walls of a classroom. The boundaries of today's classrooms are unlimited as networks bring information from around the world —voice, data, and images —directly to students.(Photograph by Alen MacWeene, Copyright 1991. Courtesy of BellSouth.)

Alabamians today have access to the world's foremost information resources through intelligent telecommunications networks. (Photograph by Chip Jamison, Copyright. Courtesy of BellSouth.)

The Birmingham Civil Rights Institute opened in 1992, the centerpiece of the city's Civil Rights District which includes the Kelly Ingram Park and the historic Sixteenth Street Baptist Church. The Institute celebrates the transformation of the nation and the world by the civil rights movement that began in Alabama. The Institute is a museum, as well as a center for research and discourse on human rights issues. (Jefferson County. Photograph by Dan Brothers. Courtesy of the Alabama Bureau of Tourism and Travel.)

**H**
Hale County, 132, 195
Handy, W. C., 110
Heflin, 127
(Cleburne Co.)
Helena, 127, 181
Henry County, 62, 72, 206
Hill, Senator Lister, 29
Hobson City, 131
Horseshoe Bend National Military Park, 7
Houston County, 60, 62, 192, 206
Houston, Governor George Smith, 25
Hunt, Governor Guy, 25
Huntingdon College, 136
Huntsville, 19, 29, 31, 41, 42, 55, 58, 89, 94, 95, 99, 113, 115, 129, 142, 155, 171, 198, 199, 207
Huntsville Arsenal, 95

**I**
Independent Blues of Selma, 36
Irondale, 84

**J**
Jackson, President Andrew, 16, 17, 20, 90, 99, 191
Jackson County, 47, 134, 206
Jacksonville, 142
Jacksonville State University, 142
Jacobs, Pattie Ruffner, 27
James, Governor Forrest "Fob," 6, 169
Jeanes Negro Rural School Fund, Anna T., 130
Jefferson County, 27, 34, 41, 43, 46, 74, 76, 80, 84, 85, 113, 116, 119, 123, 125, 130, 133, 138, 144, 152, 153, 163, 164, 165, 169, 170, 171, 176, 183, 186, 189, 196, 204, 205
Jordan Dam, 91
Jordan, Ralph "Shug," 169
Judson College, 136

**K**
Keller, Helen, 105
Kennedy, 121, 175, 195
Kilby, Governor Thomas E., 181
King, Dr. Martin Luther, Jr., 152, 157
Ku Klux Klan, 28, 125

**L**
Lake Martin, 9
Lamar County, 121, 153, 175, 195
Lange, Dorothea, 91, 192
Lauderdale County, 51, 71, 110, 161
Lawrence County, 59
Lay Dam, 92
Lee County, 61, 110, 120, 122, 143, 169, 177, 180
Lee, General Robert E., 39
Limestone County, 121, 206
Linden, 35
Little River, 13
Livingston, 141, 142, 189
Lowndes County, 16, 41, 128
Lucy, Autherine, 34

**M**
Mabila, 15
Macon County, 49, 59, 60, 141, 142, 153, 160, 172, 184, 193,
Madison County, 41, 42, 55, 89, 94, 95, 99, 115, 171, 206, 207
Marengo County, 22, 34, 70
Marion County, 64, 201
Marion Institute, 165
Marshall County, 171
Marshall Space Flight Center, George C., 95, 198
Marshall, Thurgood, 34
Martin, Thomas W., 91
Maxwell Field, 46, 47, 48, 49, 78, 80
McIntosh, William, 107
McKinley, President William, 42, 184, 189
Millerville, 132, 163
Mobile, 26, 28, 44, 45, 48, 49, 50, 57, 77, 79, 87, 90, 93, 94, 113, 114, 123, 126, 129, 132, 136, 140, 147, 152, 155, 166, 171, 172, 174, 177, 191, 198, 200, 207

Mobile County, 26, 28, 41, 48, 50, 77, 79, 87, 93, 94, 107, 108, 114, 123, 126, 140, 166, 171, 174, 194, 200, 206
Mobile River, 16, 69, 200
Monroe County, 154
Montevallo, 83, 143, 144, 189
Montgomery, 20, 21, 22, 25, 29, 34, 35, 37, 39, 41, 42, 45, 46, 47, 48, 69, 72, 75, 76, 78, 80, 81, 83, 90, 112, 113, 116, 119, 136, 142, 144, 150, 152, 155, 156, 157, 166, 167, 170, 172, 177, 184, 191, 198. 51
Montgomery County, 14, 21, 22, 25, 28, 34, 35, 39, 41, 45, 47, 48, 49, 63, 67, 72, 75, 80, 81, 89, 112, 116, 150, 156, 157, 161, 167, 170, 172, 177, 178, 186
Moore, Governor A. B., 22
Morgan County, 52, 78, 148, 177, 206
Mt. Hope, 59
Mount Olive, 177
Mt. Vernon, 194
Muscle Shoals, 68, 71, 73, 93

**N**
National League for Woman's Service, 45
Ninety-ninth Pursuit Squadron, 46, 49

**O**
Opelika, 61, 180, 198, 207

*204*

Birmingham skyline at evening from Red Mountain. (Jefferson County. Photograph by Dan Brothers. Courtesy of the Alabama Bureau of Tourism and Travel.)

Opp, 170
Orange Beach, 198
Ordinance of Secession, 22
Owen, Marie Bankhead, 7, 28
Owen, Thomas M., Jr., 14, 28, 39
Oxford, 75
Ozark, 51, 175

P
Parks, Rosa, 34
Patterson, Governor John, 33
Perry County, 165
Phenix City, 69
Pickens County, 50, 117
Pike County, 141, 163, 180
Pinson, 133
Pintala Creek, 14
Point Clear, 139
Pool, Sybil, 35
Pratt, Daniel, 21, 83, 88, 113
Prattville, 83, 87, 122, 187

R
Rainbow Division, 45, 46
Randolph County, 139
Red Level, 154
Redstone Arsenal, 94, 95
Roanoke, 191
Roosevelt, President Franklin D., 27, 29, 59, 93, 186
Russell County, 191
Russell Mills, 94
Rutan, 45

S
St. Clair County, 192
St. Stephens, 19, 129
Sansom, Emma, 187
Semmes, Admiral Raphael, 39
Selma, 18, 24, 35, 36, 39, 57, 69, 84, 113, 126, 127, 155, 180, 194, 198
Sheffield, 71, 114
Shelby County, 127, 143, 181
Shores, Arthur, 34
Simpson, Mary Lee, 104, 191, 192, 196
Sipsey River, 79
Skyline Farms, 134
Sloss-Sheffield Steel and Iron Company, 84
Southern Christian Leadership Conference, 34
Sparkman, Senator John, 29, 31
Sparks, Governor Chauncey, 31, 160
Spring Hill College, 136, 140
Styx River, 91
Sumter County, 141, 189
Sylacauga, 90, 154, 196

T
Talladega, 136
Talladega College, 142
Talladega County, 90, 100, 108, 154, 196
Tallapoosa County, 7, 9, 61, 65, 70, 74, 88, 99, 158
Tallapoosa River, 9, 16, 69, 70, 73
Tallassee, 114
Tankersley, Will Hill, 51
Tannehill, 82
Tennessee Coal, Iron and Railroad Company, 85, 88, 171
Tennessee River, 68, 69, 71, 73, 148
Tennessee-Tombigbee Waterway, 201
Tennessee Valley Authority, 29, 93
Tensaw, 16
Textile Workers Union of America, 89
Thirteenth Alabama Infantry, 102
Thirty-second Alabama Infantry, 38
Thorsby, 184
Tombigbee River, 69, 70
Troy, 87, 142
Troy State University (Troy State Normal College), 141, 142
Turner, Benjamin Sterling, 24
Tuscaloosa, 18, 20, 21, 69, 87, 94, 113, 136, 144, 166, 189, 198
Tuscaloosa County, 20, 71, 82, 95, 144, 189
Tuscumbia, 73, 105, 191
Tuskegee, 46, 142, 184
Tuskegee Airmen, 46, 49
Tuskegee University (Tuskegee Institute), 58, 59, 60, 62, 130, 141, 142, 167,184
Tutwiler, Henry, 129, 189
Tutwiler, Julia, 141, 189
Twenty-second Alabama Infantry, 102

U
University of Alabama, 7, 34, 110, 136, 142, 144, 166, 169, 189
University of Alabama at Birmingham, 142, 144
University of Alabama at Huntsville, 142
University of Montevallo, 143, 144, 189, 191
University of North Alabama, 142
University of South Alabama, 144
University of West Alabama(Livingston University, Alabama Normal School at Livingston)141,142,189

V
Vance, 95
von Braun, Wernher, 95

W
Walker County, 39, 84
Wallace, Governor George C., 31, 33, 35, 144
Wallace, Governor Lurleen Burns, 31, 35
Warrior River, 20
Washington County, 45, 160
Washington, Dr. Booker T., 130, 141, 142
Wetumpka, 69, 122
Wheeler, General Joseph, 42, 43
Williams, Hank, 177
Wilcox County, 10, 12, 45, 104, 120, 135,149, 156, 191, 192, 196
Wilmer, Bishop Richard Hooker, 155
Wilson Dam, 93
Wilson, President Woodrow, 26
Winston County, 39, 79
Women's Army Corps, 49
Wright Brothers, 78, 80

*205*

Alabama's agriculture is a cornerstone of the state's economy. Alabama farmers received over $2.91 billion in cash receipts from 1993 farm marketings. Alabama poultry and poultry products accounted for 54 percent of the total receipts. Cattle and calves ranked second with 13 percent. Greenhouse and nursery products were third, followed by cotton, peanuts, hogs, vegetables, dairy products, soybeans, catfish, fruits and nuts, corn, hay, and wheat. In 1994, Alabama had forty-six thousand farms that sold at least $1,000 or more of agricultural products during the year. In 1993, Limestone County produced the most cotton, Houston County the most peanuts, Madison County the most soybeans and wheat, Jackson County the most corn, and Henry County the most sorghum. Cullman County recorded the most beef cattle, broilers, and eggs and Morgan County the most milk cows. DeKalb County produced the most hogs and pigs. In 1993, Chilton County harvested 9,104,000 pounds of peaches, and Mobile and Baldwin counties combined to produce over 10,500,000 pounds of pecans. (Courtesy of Alabama Farmers Federation.)

The Hampton Cove course in Huntsville offers dramatically changing terrain and the Appalachian Mountains in the background. The Highlands Course features thousands of Japanese black pines, oaks, dogwoods, and crepe myrtles. The River Course is laid out on former soybean fields in the flooded plain of the Flint River, a throwback to the way courses were built long ago. (Madison County. Courtesy of the SunBelt Golf Corporation.)

The Robert Trent Jones Golf Trail is the largest golf course construction project ever attempted anywhere in the world. Funded as an investment by the Retirement Systems of Alabama, it features eighteen courses at seven facilities that stretch from the foothills of the Appalachians to the Gulf of Mexico. All of the courses—located in Huntsville, Gadsden, Birmingham, Auburn/Opelika, Greenville, Dothan, and Mobile—were designed by Robert Trent Jones Sr., one of only two course designers in the World Golf Hall of Fame. The courses all partake of the dramatic natural diversity of the topography of the state. In 1994, the Trail was named as the best public golf facilities in America by *Diversions Magazine.*

(below) *Golf Digest* named the Cambrian Ridge course in Greenville as the third best new public course in America in 1994. Golfers can enjoy gently rolling fairways, cathedral-like loblolly pines, and water-fronted greens. (Butler County. Courtesy of the SunBelt Golf Corporation.)

# about the authors

Leah Rawls Atkins is a native of Birmingham and holds a Ph.D. degree in history from Auburn University. She has taught history at Auburn, the University of Alabama at Birmingham, and Samford University. She is the director emeritus of the Auburn University Center for the Arts and Humanities and an adjunct professor in the History Department. Atkins has published in the fields of nineteenth-century Southern and Alabama history, and she is co-author of *Alabama: The History of a Deep South State*, published by the University of Alabama Press in 1994. She is past president and currently secretary of the Alabama Historical Association.

William Warren Rogers was raised in Greenville, Alabama, where he attended public schools. He graduated from Auburn University in 1950, received his master's degree there in 1951, and his Ph.D. from the University of North Carolina at Chapel Hill in 1959. He is a professor of history at Florida State University. Professor Rogers has written a number of articles and books on Southern history, specializing in the period since 1865 and concentrating on Alabama, Georgia, and Florida. His most recent book, *Alabama: The History of a Deep South State*, was co-authored with Robert David Ward, Leah Rawls Atkins, and Wayne Flynt.

Robert David Ward, who was born in Montevallo, is professor emeritus of history at Georgia Southern University. His undergraduate and masters degrees are from Auburn University. He received his Ph.D from the University of North Carolina at Chapel Hill. With Atkins, Rogers, and Flynt, he is co-author of *Alabama: The History of a Deep South State*.

Alice Knierim is assistant director for field services at the Alabama Department of Archives and History in Montgomery. She has a B.A. from Emory University and a M.A. from the University of Kentucky. Ms. Knierim is active in and has served on the councils of several public history and museum related state and national organizations.